Principles of conveyancing

Charles Watkins

Title: Principles of conveyancing

Author: Charles Watkins

This is an exact replica of a book published in 1800. The book reprint
was manually improved by a team of professionals, as opposed
to automatic/OCR processes used by some companies. However,
the book may still have imperfections such as missing pages, poor
pictures, errant marks, etc. that were a part of the original text. We
appreciate your understanding of the imperfections which can not
be improved, and hope you will enjoy reading this book.

 Book Renaissance
www.ren-books.com

PRINCIPLES

OF

CONVEYANCING:

DESIGNED FOR THE USE OF

STUDENTS.

WITH AN

INTRODUCTION ON THE STUDY

OF

THAT BRANCH OF LAW.

―――――

BY CHARLES WATKINS, ESQ.
OF THE MIDDLE TEMPLE.

―――――

LONDON:

PRINTED FOR J. BUTTERWORTH, FLEET-STREET;

BY G. WOODFALL, NO. 22, PATERNOSTER-ROW.

―――

1800.

TO

THE HONOURABLE

SIR FRANCIS BULLER, BART.

ONE OF THE JUSTICES OF

HIS MAJESTY's COURT OF COMMON PLEAS,

THE FOLLOWING ESSAY

ON THE

PRINCIPLES OF CONVEYANCING,

IS

MOST RESPECTFULLY INSCRIBED

BY

HIS OBLIGED AND

OBEDIENT SERVANT,

CHARLES WATKINS.

CONTENTS.

CONTENTS.

BOOK II.

Of Conveyances as they relate to Estates.

BOOK III.

Of Conveyances with Refpect to Parties.

INTRODUCTION.

AMONG the many difcouragements which attend the ftudy of the law, there is none more obvious, or more generally complained of, than the want of method and direction.

To take a young perfon from an univerfity or a fchool, where his mind has been occupied with other purfuits, and to tofs him headlong in the practice of the law, wholly unprepared, or with little preparation, for fo arduous a ftudy, is in itfelf fo abfurd, that we can only wonder at its occurrence.

What muft be the embarraffment of fuch a perfon, amid bufinefs of fuch

nicety

nicety as to call forth the full exertion of the veteran in practice ?—It is folly to expect from the human mind what a moment's reflection would tell us it would be impofsible for the human mind to perform. Conveyancing is not intuitive any more than the mathematics. The mind cannot draw conclufions without having been previoufly furnifhed with premifes. And however the individual may be prepoffeffed in favour of a peculiar mode of ftudy, there are, and, while the human mind continues what it is, there muft be general rules which ought to be attended to in the acquiring of knowledge.

We muft be fenfible that we can act with greater energy in proportion as our attention is confined. That attention becomes weakened as it becomes divided. We muft analyze in order to comprehend with accuracy. We muft underftand the caufe before we can embrace its confe-

quences.

quences. It fhould feem to follow, therefore, that in law, as in other fciences, we fhould begin with firft principles, and form a general outline before we defcend to the *minutiæ.*

A general outline the mind can eafily embrace, and the general principles of law it can eafily remember. When acquainted with a whole we may difcern the fymmetry of the parts; but an infulated pofition will appear arbitrary, and its connection will not be feen. As difficulties arife, or new matter prefents itfelf, a general principle will afford us a rallying point; and we fhall find ourfelves poffeffed of premifes from which we may argue.

To a general outline and to general principles, then, fhould the ftudent be at firft confined. To rufh into mifcellaneous and unconnected reading is to.divide

vide and diftract the intellect; is to weary the powers of the mind with un-neceffary, and with ufelefs, exertion. · It is to contradict the fuggeftions of common fenfe and experience, and to violate the rules which nature herfelf has im-pofed.

But, in direct defiance of principles fo obvious, how often do we fee *Coke upon Littleton* or a volume of Reports put into the hands of a young perfon on his en-tering upon the profefsion ! ' From the mifcellaneous nature of fuch writings, an idea is often effaced as foon - as · it is formed. The mind is hurried from fub-ject to fubject, without being fuffered to dwell fufficiently upon any. Points of the greateft nicety and learning the moft abftrufe are fuddenly prefented to the view of a novice, which would perhaps puzzle the ableft head of the moft ex-perienced lawyer. Deductions and con-

clufions

clufions are given when the principles from whence they flowed remain unexplained and even unknown to the ftudent.—The obfervations on *Littleton*, by Lord *Coke*, are wholly without method. Such a chaos of incoherent obfervation is by no means calculated for a regular perufal. Our attention is frequently called from an anxious confideration of a legal principle' to a differtation on the *&c.* of Littleton, to an account of Sir William Hearle, or to a quotation from Virgil or Horace. Indeed, the want of method in moft of this writer's works makes them more proper for occafional confultation than the perufal of the ftudent. His ftrange quaintnefs and excentricities may, make one fmile; but they divert the attention and withdraw it from the fubject to which we wifh it confined.

That the *Commentary upon Littleton* contains a valuable fund of Common Law learning

learning is certain: but the obfervations are thrown together without order. Great as Lord *Coke* may be, the prejudice in his favour may, perhaps, be extravagant. His induftry was aftonifhing; but he feems to have poffeffed little of the fpirit of law : and whatever might have been his legal learning, the frequent illiberality of his fentiments cannot be fufficiently reprobated*; and the ftudent ought to be cautioned againft it.

A vo-

---

* The manner in which he treated Sir Walter Raleigh may be feen in the State Trials; and will be an objeft of execration while his name fhall continue.

In Calvin's cafe (7 *Rep.* 17. a.) he fays, " All infidels (among whom he reckoned the *Jews*, 2 *Inft.* 507. are in law *perpetui inimici*, perpetual enemies, for the law prefumes not that they will be converted, that being *remota potentia*, (a remote poffibility) for between them, as with *the devils, whofe fubjefts they be*, and the Chriftian, there

is

A volume of Reports muſt, from its very nature, be full of unconnected matter; and, confequently, be improper for early reading. The report of particular cafes may, indeed, be read by the ſtudent with advantage; but they ſhould be cautiouſly pointed out for his perufal, and carefully explained.

---

is perpetual hoſtility, and can be no peace." The illiberality of Lord *Coke* with refpect to the Jews has been defervedly condemned, and held up to deteſtation, in the cafe of Omychund *v.* Barker, which is reported in a very fuperior manner by *Atkins* (vol. 1. p. 11.) and which cannot be too ſtrongly recommended to the reader's perufal. The argument of the Solicitor-General, Mr. Murray, (afterwards Lord Mansfield) is a maſter-piece of it's kind; and thofe of the Lord Chancellor (Hardwicke) and the three Chiefs who affifted him (Lee and Willes, C. J. J. and Parker, C. B.) were worthy of Chriſtians, as the fentiments of Lord Coke were difgraceful to him as a man, and much more fo as a profeſſor of the Gofpel.

The

The number of reporters and the manner in which many cafes are reported are moft ferious evils; are evils which cannot be too much lamented nor fufficiently expofed. The contradictory ftatements of the fame cafe, the confounding the arguments, nay, affertions of the counfel, with the decifions of the court, the *obiter* and extra-judicial fayings of the Judges, with the grounds of the judgment, the obfervations of the reporter with the points of the cafe, call aloud for the niceft and fevereft difcrimination.

I believe it will be found on examination, that a deference to the affertions of our predeceffors, whatever ftations thofe predeceffors might have filled, has been one of the moft certain fources of error. Perhaps there is nothing which has fo fhackled the human intellect, nothing which

which has fo retarded the progrefs of truth, nothing which has fo greatly promoted whatever is tyrannic, prepofterous, or abfurd, nothing which has fo much degraded the fpecies in the fcale of being, as a deference to individual *dicta.* The blunders of one age (and blunders have occurred in all ages) cannot warrant the blunders of another. What was once expedient may now, by reafon of a change of circumftances, be improper. To appeal to matters of fact with refpect to matters of right is, in itfelf, fo prepofterous, that we fhould have very great reafon indeed to induce us to have recourfe to it. If we muft be bound by former decifions, let thofe decifions be given by the moft unequivocal authority. Let the ftatement of facts, the decifion of the court, and the grounds and reafons of that decifion, be drawn up by a proper officer, and figned by the Judges who prefide.

Let

Let not the crude notes of the dead be brought forward to miflead the living. Let not the reputation of thofe who have left us, and who are no longer able to defend themfelves, become the prey of the fweepers of their clofets. We fhould confider that many who took notes in court did not take them with a view to publication; but that they were frequently ufhered into public merely from the rapacity or avarice of thofe who furvived. Compare *Rolle's* reports with his abridgment. Look at the undetermined cafes in *Dyer.* Confider how foon a quoted cafe becomes what is called authority, and confider how foon authority fhoulders out common fenfe. It would not be difficult to point out many inftances in which the adherence to the reports of adjudged cafes has overthrown the acknowledged principles of the law of the land, and, in effect, repealed the

folemn

folemn acts of the legiflative body*; though the Judges had fworn to adminifter the laws inftead of receiving authority to controul or refcind them. If the acts of the legiflative body become incompatible with the manners of the times, let us apply to the legiflative body for their alteration or repeal, but let not the Judges become fuperior to the legiflative body.

" *Ita lex fcripta eft,*" is the cry of many a man who would be angry with another that expreffed a doubt whether he poffeffed ratiocination. About the time of pafsing the ftatute of ufes fome wife man, in the plenitude of legal learning, declared that

---

* In the celebrated Bewdley cafe, (which has been frequently recognized *as law!*) the practice of the Court for feven years was held fuperior to an Act of Parliament! 1 *P. Wms.* 223: 2 *Str.* 755. 3 *Burr.* 1755.

there could not be an ufe upon an ufe.
This very wife declaration; which muſt
have furprifed every one who was not
fufficiently learned to have loſt his
common-fenfe, was adopted, and is ſtill
adopted ; and upon it (at leaſt chiefly)
has been built the prefent fyſtem of
ufes and truſts. Another, adopting juſt
fo much of an argument as anfwered his
purpofe, and rejecting a conclufion
which followed from the felf-fame premifes, decreed that there fhould be no
dower of a truſt; and Chancellor after
Chancellor fubmitted to this ſtrange affertion, and followed it in defiance of
every thing rational. " We are bound
by precedent," fay they : but are we
not bound by principle alfo? Can precedent releafe us from a moral obligation?

If reports of adjudged cafes be frequently found fuch as I have noticed, it
furely

furely will be fufficient to advert to them, in order to guard the ftudent from relying upon them where the reafon of the de-cifion is not apparent.

When we argue from adjudged cafes, we argue from conclufions already drawn, and not from premifes by which thofe conclufions muft be warranted. The more we are removed from thofe premifes, the greater the probability of error in our con-.clufions muft necefiarily be.

But fuppofing that a perfon fhould be fo fortunate as to be able to extract fomething comprehenfible out of *printed* contradiction, yet other contradictions may make their appearance in *manu-fcript*; and, overthrowing all his hard-earned knowledge, remind him once again of *the glorious uncertainty of the law.* Is the law of England to depend upon the private note of an individual, and to which

b 2 an

an individual only can have accefs? Is
a Judge to fay—" Lo! I have the law of
England on this point in my pocket.
Here is a note of the cafe, which contains
an exact ftatement of the whole facts,
and the decifion of my Lord *A.* or my
Lord *B.* upon them. He was a' great, a
very great man. I am bound by his decifion. All you have been reading was
erroneous. The printed books are inaccurate. I cannot go into principle. The
point is fettled by this cafe."—Under fuch
circumftances, who is to know when he is
right or when he is wrong? If conclufions
from unqueftionable principles are to be
overthrown in the laft ftage of a fuit by private *memoranda*, who can hope to become
acquainted with the laws of England?
And who, that retains any portion of ra-
tionality, would wafte his time and his
talents in fo fruitlefs an attempt? Is a
paper evidencing the law of England to
be buttoned up in the fide-pocket of a
Judge,

Judge, or to ferve for a moufe to fit upon in the dufty corner of a private library? If the law of England is to be deduced from adjudged cafes, let the reports of thofe adjudged cafes be certain, known, and authenticated. What an idea muft a foreigner form of our laws when he conceives them either founded upon, or fubject to be contradicted by, nobody knows what?

I acknowledge the utility of publifhing the folemn decifions of the Courts; but I fay again, let the reports of thofe decifions be faithfully given, and ftamped with authority; and let the grounds of fuch decifions be rational and apparent *. Let not the laws of England be picked out,

---

* It is but little confolation to fay, on the trial of a caufe, " That cafe is not law," after it has mifled half the kingdom.

b 3   like

like diamonds from a dung-hill, from among fuch crude and incoherent, fuch unintelligible and contradictory matter as now loads our fhelves. Let us ferioufly confider the evils which muft arife from fuffering abfurdity to be confecrated by ufe; and, when eftablifhed as a precedent, to interfere with, and perhaps to render nugatory, the undoubted principles of our laws.

If the laws of England are to depend upon the decifion of a Judge, we fhould remember that the decifion of a Judge may overthrow them.

However well acquainted a perfon may be with adjudged cafes, he will foon find cafes occur in practice with which thofe already decided will not altogether accord. In fuch circumftance he can only have recourfe to principle. The necefsity of an acquaintance with principle, there-

forc, is too apparent to be further in-
fifted on.

Another clafs of writings which the
ftudent fhould avoid, or, at leaft, read
with extreme caution, is that of detached
arguments on cafes which have been adjudged. Arguments thus publifhed, when
prefented under the fanction of general
reputation, and crouded with a profufion
of legal reference, are too often calculated
to miflead. The ftudent muft not be fa-
tisfied with affertion, or carried away by
the name of an author. If he cannot
confront argument with argument, and
receive the neceffary *data* on *both* fides of
the queftion, he fhould fufpend his judge-
ment: he muft not decide upon *ex parte*
evidence. Befides, fuch arguments are,
for the moft part, on points of much
nicety, and which feldom arife; and he
fhould defer the confideration of fuch till
he has made himfelf mafter of principles

b 4   more

more general, and of propofitions more obvious and evident.

When fuccefs has attended a peculiar
mode of ftudy, it may be reafonable to
fuppofe it to be juft, and warrantable to
recommend it to others. I would, therefore, advife the ftudent to begin with a.
general outline: he may fill it up at his
leifure, as he may find himfelf prepared
for the undertaking: to confine himfelf
at firft ftrictly to principles; and, when
he meets with technical terms, to be con-
tent with a mere explanation, and not
purfue the fubject of that term any further, as it will only withdraw his attention from that which he meant to purfue.
It is the great fault of our Law Dic-
tionaries, generally, that they partake too
much of the nature of abridgments. But
a dictionary and an abridgment are very
different things, and ought to be kept
apart. It is much to be wifhed that a

Law

Law Dictionary might be given which would comprehend merely the terms of art, and thofe obfolete words which occur in old legal or hiftorical writers.

His general books may be *Finche's Law*, *Blackstone's Commentaries*, *Wynne's Enomus*, *Hale's Common Law*, *Reeves's History*, *Sullivan's Lectures*, *Dalrymple on Feudal Property*, *Littleton* (without the Commentary), the Freehold part of *Gilbert's Tenures*, Select Notes of Mr. *Butler* to *Co. Litt. Touchstone*, and *Fonblanque on Equity*, with *Francis's Maxims*.

Having gained a general view of the Law, and being taught to divide his fubject, he may purfue it as far as his inclination may lead him. He may go up to *Puffendorf* or *Grotius*, or down to a volume of reports, or the fleeting publications of the day.

I re-

I recommend the Commentaries of *Blackstone* as a general book. The intention of that ingenious writer was to give a comprehenfive outline; and when we confider the multiplicity of doctrine which he embraced, the civil, the criminal, the theoretical and practical, branches of the Law, we muft confefs the hand of a mafter. But in the *minutiæ* he is frequently, very frequently inaccurate. He fhould, therefore, be read with caution. The ftudent in reading him will often require explanation and correction from him whofe duty it is to inftruct.

Noy's Maxims, in all the editions, are too incorrect to be entrufted in the ftudent's hands. *Perkins* has too many quæries; though *Perkins* may be gone through with advantage, if accompanied with oral explanation.

The

, The following pages have been alſo found to yield afsiſtance to the ſtudent; and they are now preſented to the world in the hope that they may be ſerviceable to others. The mode of reading them was this:—The ſtudent, after being acquainted with ſome general books (as before recommended), read the work entirely through, that he might form a view of the whole. He then began again, and read chapter by chapter; confulting the books, or portions of books referred to, but confining himſelf ſtrictly to the fubject of the chapter immediately before him; and the whole was accompanied with oral explanation whenever he felt himſelf at a lofs. He paufed between the chapters, when the connection was not immediate, that there might be no concufsion of ideas, or that an idea formed on one ſubject might as little as pofsible be effaced by an idea on another.

The

The ftudy of the laws of a country, and efpecially of laws which have been accumulating for many, many centuries, muft neceffarily be attended with labour. But we fhould not intimidate the ftudent at the threfhold with unneceffary embarraffment. Much labour may be prevented by method, and much difguft by a favourable imprefsion.

To prove that the profefsion of the law is an honourable profefsion, we muft fhew it to be enlarged in its principles, and liberal in its practice. To have gentlemen and men of genius in the profefsion, we muft fhew the profefsion to be fuch as a gentleman and a man of genius may purfue.

Law fhould be confidered as a moral fcience, as the rule of rational and accountable beings. The profefsion of the Law was inftituted merely for the furtherance
ance

ance of juſtice and the prefervation of right; ſhall we pervert it, then, to the fupprefsion of what it was ordained to fupport? Shall we reprefent it as incompatible with any thing that is liberal, or manly, or ufeful? If the profefsion can only be purfued by abandoning the rigid dictates of moral rectitude, the nicer feelings of humanity, or the exertion of the nobler powers of the mind, it is a profefsion which it would be criminal in man to purfue. The conduct of fome of its profeffors has, indeed, fubjected it to much contempt; and from thofe who muſt regard it with contempt it is folly to expect admiration: and the conduct of many who profefs themfelves its friends, tends but little to remove the odium it has ſhared.

It is ridiculous to hear a perfon, who boaſts that his profefsion is *an honorary* profefsion, talking inceffantly of his fees.

It

It is ridiculous to hear a perfon who, in a court of juftice, wilfully embarraffes a witnefs for the fake of gaining his caufe, right or wrong, call his profefsion an *honourable one.* ·It is ridiculous to hear a perfon talking of *the honour* of his profefsion, who receives a fum of money for difcovering a loop-hole in a title merely to enable his employer to creep through, that he might refcind a contract which he had entered into with his eyes open, and which every principle of moral rectitude would oblige him to perform.

We may talk as much as we pleafe about the honour of a profefsion of which a conduct like this forms a part; but, while a conduct like this forms a part of a profefsion, no man of common honefty or of common fenfe can ceafe to regard it with contempt.

But

But by ſhowing that a conduct like this
is only the perverſion of individuals;—
that the profeſsion, ſo far from requiring
it, is diſgraced by a conduct like this;—
that it affords field for the exertion of the
moſt tranſcendent abilities, and the moſt
benevolent inclinations;—that it is com-
patible with whatever elevates or adorns
the character of man,—can we only hope
that the profeſsion will own the Good
and the Great.—It is by ſuch means only
that it can retain its wonted place in the
ſcale of ſcience, and be rendered worthy
of the human mind.

If the day be not yet come, the day is
very faſt approaching, when knowledge
ſhall be juſtly appreciated; when ſyſte-
matic pedantry ſhall no more acquire the
reputation of learning; when thoſe lite-
rary purſuits, which incumber the me-
mory without calling forth the exertion
of

of intellect, or amending the heart, shall
be defervedly reprobated ; when prejudice
shall melt away before the genial beams
of investigation and truth ; and when
learning shall only be esteemed as it becomes subservient to the virtue, and, of
consequence, to the happiness of man-
kind.

PRINCIPLES

OF

CONVEYANCING, &c.

BOOK I.

OF ESTATES AND INTERESTS, AS THEY RELATE TO CONVEYANCES.

CHAP. I.

OF AN ESTATE AT WILL.

AN Eftate at Will is not bounded by definite limits with refpect to time; but as it orignated in mutual agreement, fo it depends upon the concurrence of both parties. As it depends upon the will of both, the diffent of either may determine it. Such an eftate or intereft cannot, confequently, be the fubject of convey‑ance.

2 *Blackft.*
Comm. ch. 9.
p. 145, to the
end.
Litt. b. 1.
ch. 8. and the
Comment.

B

ance. Could the *leſſee* (for he is not a *termor*, as a termor is co-relative with a *term*, or *definite* event,) convey the premiſes to another, he would determine *his own will* to hold. He himſelf would be no longer a tenant; for he cannot be a tenant and not a tenant at the ſame time; and by the transfer he would part with *his own intereſt.* As the tenancy *is at will*, it muſt, of conſequence, be at the will of the leſſor as well as of the leſſee. Now, if the transferree could become a tenant, it would be independently of the will of the leſſor, and conſequently would not be a tenant at *his* will, and conſequently it would not be a tenancy at will at all, as the will muſt be in ſuch caſes *reciprocal.* Should the leſſee introduce a ſtranger into the tenancy *with* the aſſent of the leſſor, it would not be a transfer of the *leſſee's* intereſt or eſtate, for *his* intereſt or eſtate would be by the very act *determined*; but a *new* eſtate at will would be created, ſince the original leſſee would relinquiſh or abdicate *his* intereſt or eſtate, and the ſtranger would take an eſtate, by the immediate

diate act of the leffor, which had never been in the original leffee.

But as it is reafonable that a perfon fhould reap what he has fown, and as the greateft part, if not the whole, of the year, is requifite for the purpofes of agriculture in its prefent ftate, the law does not favour an eftate at will; and if the rent be referved yearly or half-yearly, it frequently takes the circumftance as evidence of a *term* ; *i. e.* of a leafe for a year, or from year to year. Yet as fuch a prefumption is merely for the furtherance of juftice, if fuch conftruction would, on the contrary, be productive of wrong, fuch conftruction cannot take place, according to the maxim that a conftruction of law, as fuch, fhall do injury to none. As, for inftance, if a leafe from year to year would work a *forfeiture*, there can be no reafon for conftruing fuch a demife a leafe for a year rather than an eftate at will.

Bull. Nifi Prius, 84. 2. J. Blackft. Rep. 1173. 2 Bl. Comm. 147.

But a leffee at will, though he cannot transfer his own intereft, is capable of accepting a releafe of the inheritance from

Litt. Sect. 460. Co. Litt. 270. b.

B 2   his

his leſſor, on ſuch leſſee's entry into the premiſes: for he has a notorious poſſeſſion on entry, and the reverſion or inheritance may be releaſed to ſuch an one.

The ſtudent ſhould, however, be informed that there are caſes in which it has been held, that an eſtate at will does not, at this day, in reality exiſt. But, in order to prevent his being miſled, the following obſervations are ſubjoined, and recommended to his conſideration.

The exiſtence of an eſtate at will was acknowledged in the caſe of Doe *d.* Bree *v.* Lees, 2 *J. Blackſt. Rep.* 1171. *Bull. Niſi Pri.* 85.—2 *Bl. Comm.* 146.

An eſtate ſtrictly at will was, however, in ſome inſtances, found inconvenient, and accordingly the courts did not favour it; but if the caſe admitted of a different conſtruction, they gave it a different conſtruction, and declared the demiſe a demiſe mife from year to year. They did not pronounce it an eftate at will, and deny it the effential of an eftate at will: this was a refinement in abfurdity which future days were to acquire. But they faid This demife is *not* an eftate at will, but from year to year.

A clafs of cafes next came that cut the matter fhorter. Inftead of determining when the admifsion of an eftate of will was advifable, or not advifable, they denied its very exiftence. See 5 *Durnf. & Eaft*, 471, Doe *d.* Rigge *v.* Bell.—8 *D. & E.* 3. Clayton *v.* Blakey—and fee 3 *Burr.* 1609, in Timmins *v.* Rowlinfon.

In Doe *d.* Rigge *v.* Bell, Lord Kenyon is reprefented as faying, " Though the agreement (for feven years by parol) be *void* by the ftatute of frauds *as to the duration of the leafe*, it muft regulate the terms on which *the tenancy fubfifts* in *other* refpects, as to the rent, the *time of the year when the tenant is to quit*, &c. Now in this cafe it was agreed that the defendant fhould quit at Candlemas, and though the

agreement

agreement is *void as to the number of years for which the defendant was to hold*, if the leſſor *chuſe* to determine the tenancy *before* the expiration of the ſeven years, he *can only put an end to it at Candlemas*."

Now it would be no common exertion of the human intellect to conceive how a tenancy could *ſubſiſt* in *other* reſpects, or in *any* reſpect, *after its duration had ceaſed by a poſitive act of parliament*; or how the leſſor ſhould not be at liberty to determine the tenancy at his pleaſure, after it was made a leaſe at *his* will as well as at the will of the leſſee, by the ſame act of parliament; or how it could be an eſtate at will at all, if the leſſor could *not determine it till a certain fixed period*. If the leſſor ſhould *not* have choſen to determine the tenancy *before* the expiration of the ſeven years, was it to be a tenancy for ſeven years in defiance of the act of parliament? Such an eſtate muſt be either an eſtate at will, or *not* an eſtate at will. If it *be* an eſtate at will, then it may, from the very nature of the thing, *be determinable at any time*; and if it be *not* an

                             eſtate

eftate at will, then the ftatute of frauds and perjuries is, as to this point, in effect, repealed by judges who had fworn to adminifter the laws of which that ftatute formed a part. For it would be the very apex of abfurdity to fay that, though it *be* an eftate at will *in other refpects*, yet it is *not* an eftate at *will with refpect to its duration*; for if it be *not* an eftate at *will with refpect to its duration*, it can be *no eftate at will at all.* And it certainly can be no eftate at will with refpect to its duration, if it *be not determinable till a given period.*

The ftatute of frauds exprefsly declares, that fuch a demife fhould " have the force and effect of a leafe or eftate *at will* ONLY, and fhould not, either in law or equity, *be deemed or taken to have* ANY OTHER, *or* GREATER *force or effect, any confideration for making fuch parol leafe or eftate, or any former*" (the ftatute could not, from the very nature of the thing, provide againft any future) " law or ufage to the contrary notwithftanding." Now, in an unqualified manner to affert that that ef-

tate

tate which the ſtatute poſitively declared
SHOULD *be an eſtate* AT WILL ONLY, *and*
SHOULD NOT, EITHER IN LAW OR EQUI-
TY, BE DEEMED OR TAKEN TO HAVE
ANY OTHER OR GREATER EFFECT, ſhould
NOT *be an eſtate at will only*, but SHOULD
be deemed and taken to have ANOTHER AND
GREATER EFFECT, is certainly very bold,
if not as certainly very wrong.

In Clayton *v.* Blakey, Lord *Kenyon* is
made to ſay, " The meaning of the ſtatute was that ſuch an agreement *ſhould
not operate* AS A TERM. But what was
then conſidered as a tenancy at will, has
ſince been properly conſtrued to enure *as
a tenancy from year to year.*" Now, what
is *a tenancy from year to year* but a *term ?*
In Doe *d.* Rigge *v.* Bell, his Lordſhip ex-
preſly held that the landlord could not
determine the tenancy *till the end of the
year.* But if the tenancy was not determinable *till a definite period*, it is humbly
apprehended that A TERM *did exiſt*, contrary to the ſtatute in that caſe made and
provided, whatever his Lordſhip may be
pleaſed to ſay to the contrary of that ſtatute

in any wife notwithstanding. For it would be confounding of ideas, it would be an abuse of language, it would be an insult to common sense, to affirm that an estate of a *definite duration* was *not* a *term*; or that an estate at *will* was *independent on volition*.

It seems indisputably laid down that if, on the escheat of a copyhold, the lord had leased the premises so escheated *at will*, he might grant those premises again by copy; but if he had granted them for *a term* their demisable property would have been for ever gone. The reason of the distinction was evidently this: if the premises were *at will* they were always demisable, *as the lord might determine the leafe at his pleasure*; and so *was always at liberty to demise if he had chosen to do so.* If the premises were leased for *a term*, the lord *could not during the existence of that term demise the premises to another.* In this latter case, therefore, the premises were *not* demisable by copy, being already demised for a common law interest; for when it is said that it is essential to a grant of copyholds

copyholds that they muft be either demifed or demifable, it means, manifeftly, that they muft be either demifed or demifable *by copy*, and not that they be demifed or demifable in any other way.

Whether the premifes were leafed by *deed*, or *parol*, made no difference in this refpect: for the only queftion was, whether *a term*, or *fuch an eftate which the lord could not refcind at his pleafure*, did or did not exift? If fuch a term *did* exift, then, *during fuch term*, the lands were *not* demifable; but if *no period had occurred at which the lands were not demifable*, in cafe the lord had chofen to demife them, *then* the property of the land was *not loft*.

Suppofe, therefore, that the lord fhould, at this day, make fuch a leafe of fuch efcheated lands as would have been a leafe at will before the ftatute of frauds, the queftion would be, whether fuch a leafe would, or would not, prevent him from granting thofe lands by copy of court-roll?—But, before this queftion can be determined, a previous one muft be folved, namely, whether

ther

ther ſuch a leaſe be, at this time, *a leaſe at will*, or *not a leaſe at will?*

Now ſome of the caſes which have been cited, abſolutely deny the exiſtence of an eſtate at will; and ſay that that eſtate, which formerly was an eſtate at will, is now an eſtate from year to year, and only to be determined at the end of the year; and if ſo, it muſt follow of necefsity, that *till* the end of the year the premiſes are *not* demiſable by copy; and, by conſequence, that the demiſable property of the premiſes *is loſt*, as if it ceaſe for a moment, it would be gone for ever.

An eſtate at will, they tell us, can, at this day, exiſt only *notionally*. Now, can a *notional* eſtate at will, or an eſtate in *idea*, counteract a *term in fact?* Or will they tell us, that though it be *not* an eſtate at will, yet *that it ſhall have the properties of an eſtate at will*, and ſo the demiſable quality of the lands be *ſuppoſed* to continue? This would be a *notional* quality of an eſtate with a witneſs. This would be to ſay that a thing *is* what *it is not*; or that

that it ſhall *have properties inconſiſtent with its nature.*

But, on the other hand, if we conſider that the courts endeavoured to conſtrue thoſe eſtates to be terms from year to year, rather than to be eſtates at will, merely for the purpoſes of civil convenience, we may conclude that ſuch conſtruction ought not to take place when an inconvenience does not exiſt, or where a convenience to one party would *work a wrong to another* ; and, conſequently, that an eſtate at will *may*, and *actually does, exiſt at preſent* ; and, conſequently, that *lands may be granted by copy, though ſo leaſed by the lord to another perſon.*

If this be acknowledged, we ſhall be able to diſpenſe with a great deal of very learned confuſion, and be neither obliged to deny thoſe principles which cannot be diſproved, nor to incumber them with unneceſſary nonſenſe.

CHAP. II.

OF A TERM OF YEARS.

THE next eſtate, with reſpect to the duration of intereſt, is that which the law denominates *a term*; and it is ſo denominated becauſe its duration is *abſolutely defined*. The duration of an eſtate at will is dependent upon *the pleaſure of each party*; and an eſtate for life, in tail, or in fee, is *uncertain* in its duration, as its continuance is dependent upon an uncertain event; that is, upon the death of the individual, or the extinction or failure of heirs, either ſpecial or general. Hence, then, muſt a term, from its very nature, have a certain beginning, or definite commencement, and a certain or definite period beyond which it cannot laſt. But, however ſhort its continuance be deſigned, it is a TERM, and is called a *term for years*.

2 *Bl. Comm.* c. 9. ſ. 1. p. 140—5. & c. 20. p. 317. *Litt.* b. 1. c. 7. & the *Comment.* *Touchſt.* 266. ch. 14. *Bacon's Abr.* tit. Leaſe.

But,

But, though it be effential to its very exiftence that there be a time abfolutely prefixed *beyond which it cannot continue*, yet it may be made fubject to a condition for its determination before the period prefixed: as for 99 years, *provided A. B. lives fo long.* Here, if *A. B.* die before the 99 years expire, the term fhall ceafe; but though *A. B.* fhould furvive the 99 years, the leafe, on the expiration of the 99 years, would be abfolutely at an end.

This eftate is ufually entitled *a demife,* or *leafe*; and the proper words of creation are thofe of " demife, leafe, and to farm " let;" though it may be created by other means, as by bargain and fale, though See the next without enrollment. It only relates to Chapter. the *poffefsion,* and does not affect the *feifin* of the lands. It is what the law calls a *chattel intereft,* and is not an eftate of freehold, though it be for 10,000 years. Hence, if it be wifhed that *A. B.* fhould enjoy certain premifes while he lives, it fhould be enquired into, whether it be the intention of the parties that the eftate of *A. B.* fhould have the properties of a frechold or

not;

not; as to fupport a contingent remainder;
to have the right of election of members
of parliament, &c. If it *be*, the eftate
may be limited to *A. B. and his afsigns
during his life*; if it be *not*, it fhould be
limited to *A. B. and his afsigns, for a certain number of years, provided the faid A. B.
fhall fo long live.*

·´ As this eftate affects only the poffefsion
and not the feifin, it may be made to
commence *in futuro*, as from Michaelmas-
day next. But, on the demife of a term,
no eftate is vefted in the leffee; it only
gives him a right of entry; and, till he
actually enter, he has only an *intereffe
termini*. He cannot, *before* entry, receive
a *confirmation* * or *releafe* † from the leffor;
nor can he *furrender* ‡ his intereft, except
by a furrender in law, as by accepting another leafe incompatible with the exiftence
of the firft.

An eftate for years is afsignable, unlefs
there be an exprefs condition or provifion
in the leafe to reftrict the power of alienation which the law gives; and fuch affignment

marginal notes:
5 *Co.* 123. b.
Saffyn's cafe.

* *Co. Litt.*
296. a. & n.
(2.)
† *Ib.* 270. b.
‡ *Ib.* 338. a.

*Doct. & Stud.
27. Dial.* 1
ch. 8.

signment may be made even before the *Co.Litt.46.a.* leslee enter, as an *intereffe termini* may be granted over. Or if a leafe be made to *two*, one may releafe to the other before entry.

And as a leslee may grant over his *whole term*, fo he may make an under-leafe of *a part* of his intereft. As if he have a term of ten years, he may under-let for five; and the diftinction between an afsignment and an under-leafe is, where the leslee parts with his *whole* intereft, and where *not*; in the *latter* cafe it is an *under-leafe*, in the *former* an *afsignment*. In an afsignment, the operative words are, " afsigned, transferred, and fet over;" and in an under-leafe, the fame words are ufed as in the original one.

Touchft. 300. ch. 17. 2 *Bl. Comm.* 326. *Co. Litt.* 337. b. 338. on fect. 636.

On the entry of the leslee, he may furrender to his leslor, either by a furrender in deed or in law. On a furrender in deed, the operative words are, " doth furrender, " yield up, and for ever quit claim," and to fuch furrender it is advifable to make the leslor a party, and that he execute the

3   deed,

deed, that his affent may be apparent.—
A furrender in law is, as before obferved,
the acceptance of another leafe incompatible with the firft.

But if a leffee for twenty years under- *Touchf.* 301.
leafe for ten years, he cannot, by furren-
dering up his original leafe, deftroy the
under-leafe for ten years, as it would be
manifeftly unjuft that he fhould fruftrate
his own grant.

By the Statute of Frauds (29 *Car.* II.
c. 3.) no fuch term (except it does not
exceed three years from the making of it,
and whereon the rent referved fhall amount
to two-thirds, at leaft, of the full improved
value of the thing demifed), fhall be
created, afsigned, granted, or furrendered,
unlefs by deed or note in writing, figned
by the party or his agent, or by act or
operation of law.

An eftate for years may be *devifed*, or *Harg.* n. (5.)
limited *by way of truft*, to one for life; to *Co. Litt.*
and, after his deceafe, to another; or to a 2 *Fearne,* 144.
perfon *and the heirs of his body:* but the &c.

c   perfon

perfon taking the preceding, limitation for years or life cannot defeat the limitation over; while the whole property in the term will veft abfolutely in the perfon who takes under that limitation which, if it were of freehold property, would give an *expref́s* eftate tail, without any act done by him, and the limitations over will be effectually defeated.

1 *Durnf. &
Eaft.* 596,
Doe & Lyde.
2 *Fearne,*231,
&c.

But no limitations are allowed of terms of years which would render them unalienable beyond a life or lives in being, and twenty-one years afterwards,

CHAP. III.

OF AN ESTATE OF FREEHOLD.

ESTATES *at will* and *for years* are confidered by the law as only *chattel* interefts.
An eftate for *one's own life*, or the *life of*
another perfon, or any *greater* eftate, is
deemed an eftate of *freehold*. In the tenant
of the *latter* eftate the feudal poffefsion or
fcifin is vefted; and the tenants of the *for-*
mer are regarded as only the bailiffs or
farmers of their refpective leffors. Hence
livery of feifin muft be given on the creation
of an eftate of *freehold*, though it cannot
be given on the creation of an eftate at will
or for years only, as the perfon intended
to hold at will or for years is not to be put
into the *feifin*, which muft remain in his
leffor; for if livery *had been* given, a *free-*
hold, of necefsity, would have paffed at

2 *Bl. Comm.*
143, &c.
Sulliv. Lect.
vi.
1 *Burr.* 107.
&c.
Butl. n. (1.)
to *Co. Litt.*
266. b.

c 2   common

common law*. The tenant for life, or the immediate tenant of the freehold, is to anſwer to the *præcipe* of ſtrangers, and to render to the lord the returns of the feud; and hence it is that an eſtate of freehold was not ſuffered to commence *in futuro*, as there muſt have been ſuch an immediate tenant in actual exiſtence.

---

* But ſince the Statute of Frauds, a freehold cannot paſs without writing.

CHAP. IV.

OF AN ESTATE *POUR AUTRE VIE.*

An Eſtate *pour autre vie* is 'an eſtate of *2 Bl. Comm.* *freehold*, though it is the loweſt or leaſt *120. 258. Litt. b. 1.* eſtate of freehold which the law acknow- *ſ. 56. 57. & Co. Litt. 41.* ledges. An eſtate for the life of *another* is b. &c. not ſo great as an eſtate for *one's* OWN LIFE. If *A.* have an eſtate for his own life, with *Co. Litt. 41. b. 42. a.* remainder to *B.* for the life of *B. A.* is capable of taking a ſurrender from *B.*—A *præcipe quod reddat* will lie againſt a tenant *pour autre vie*; for he, *being tenant of the freehold*, muſt anſwer to the claims of. ſtrangers; and hence it cannot be created to commence *in futuro.*

This eſtate, being an eſtate of freehold, muſt be created by ſome mode of conveyance which will paſs the freehold in

poſſeſſion;

poſſeſsion; and may be transferred, that is, conveyed, during the lives of the *celles que vies*, by the common mode of convey- ' ing freeholds.   It may alſo be ſurrendered to the immediate reverſioner, though that reverſioner be only tenant for his own life.

If an eſtate for the lives of *A. B.* and *C.* had been conveyed to *D.* without more, and *D.* had died, living *celles que vies,* the perſon who firſt entered might have enjoyed the lands during the lives of *A. B.* and *C.* But now, by the ſtatutes of *Car.* II. and *Geo.* II. *D.* may diſpoſe of the eſtate by his laſt will (to be executed according to the Statute of Frauds, it being an eſtate of freehold), or, if he die inteſtate, it ſhall go to his executors or adminiſtrators, and be diſtributed among the next kin.

29 Car. II.
c. 3. ſ. 12.
14 Geo. II.
c. 20.

Carth. 376.
Oldham *v.*
Pickering.
Ratl.'n. to *Co.*
Litt. Index,
tit. Dower.

But though this be an eſtate of freehold, it may be limited to *D.* his *executors and adminiſtrators,* as well as to *D.* and his *heirs*; for the ſucceſſors of *D. take as ſpecial occupants,* and not by deſcent.   And this mode of limitation is often preferable, as

it

it frequently faves the premifes or eftate
from the inconveniences of a minority.

An eftate *pour autre vie* may be limited *Harg.* n. (5.)
over *by way of remainder*; and, in effect, to *Co. Litt.* 20. a.
be entailed. But thofe who have interefts 2 *Fearne,* 309, &c.
in the nature of an eftate tail may bar their
iffue, and all remainders over, by alienation, without fine or recovery, as by leafe
and releafe, furrender, &c. and the having
iffue is not effential, as in the cafe of a conditional fee at common law.

CHAP. V.

OF AN ESTATE FOR LIFE.

Litt. f. 56—
57.
*Co.Litt.*41.b.
2 *Bl. Comm.*
120.
By an eftate *for life*, generally, is under-ftood an eftate for one's own life, and not for the life of another.

Like that, however, it cannot be made to commence *in futuro*, it being an eftate *of freehold*; and, for the fame reafon, it muft be created or transferred by livery of feifin, leafe and releafe, bargain and fale enrolled, &c. or be furrendered to him in reverfion.

CHAP. VI.

OF AN ESTATE IN DOWER.

DOWER is an eftate *for life*, which the law gives the widow in the *third part* of the *lands and tenements* of which the huf-band was *folely feized, at any time during the coverture*, of an eftate in *fee* or in *tail*, in *poffefsion*, and to which eftate in the lands and tenements *the iffue of fuch widow might, by pofsibility, have inherited.* 2 *Bl. Comm.* 129. *Litt. b.* 1. *c.* 5. & the *Commen. Pref. on Eft.* c. 7. *p.* 536.

This eftate, though created by act of law, may be conveyed or prevented by the act of the party.

Before afsignment and actual entry, the freehold is not in the widow; and, by con-fequence, the mode of pafsing her claim differs before and after entry.

5

Before

Before entry she has only a *right*, which must be conveyed by *releaſe*, and that to the *perſon in poſſeſsion of the lands*, as to him only a releaſe of right can be made.— *After* entry, the poſſeſsion or freehold of her third is in herſelf; and, conſequently; the proper mode of conveyance *to the per-ſon immediately in reverſion* will then be *a ſurrender*; and to *a ſtranger* it may be con-veyed by feoffment, with livery *(ſecundum formam chartæ)*, leaſe and releaſe, or bar-gain and ſale enrolled.

1 *Cruiſe.* 179.
2 *Ibid.* 96.
237.
Pigg. Rec. 66.
123. 195.
Harg. N. (C.)
to *Co. Litt.*
121. a.
Plowd. 514.
Eare *v.* Snow.

During the life of her huſband the wife may paſs, or rather bar, her right to dower, by fine or recovery; which are matters of record, and in the proceſs of which ſhe is ſecretly examined, to prevent or remove the ſuſpicion of any compulſion in the huſband.

And as dower is claimable out of thoſe lands and tenements of which the huſband was ſeized AT ANY TIME DURING THE CO-VERTURE, the alienation of the huſband alone, after marriage, will not bar her claim; and, therefore, it is neceſſary that
care

care be taken in conveyances by a married man that the widow be effectually precluded from her dower (if entitled) by her joining in levying a fine, or suffering a recovery.

Again; as dower is only claimable in such lands and tenements of which the husband was *solely seized* during the coverture, in *fee-simple* or *fee-tail in possession*, several modes present themselves by which dower may be prevented or barred.

And, in the first place, it is requisite to dower that the husband be *solely* seized; and, therefore, dower is sometimes barred by conveying the estate to *the husband and another person in joint tenancy*; in which case, as the husband was not *solely* but *jointly* seized, the dower does not attach.

But this mode is very objectionable; for if the stranger or trustee die during the life of the husband, the husband will become *solely* seized, and so the end of such conveyance be defeated.

The

The next requifite is that the hufband *be feized* ; and, confequently, another mode of preventing dower is by creating *a truft*; for a court of equity has not fuffered the widow to claim her dower in a truft-eftate.

But this mode is alfo objectional, as it puts the legal freehold out of the hufband.

A third requifite to dower is that the hufband muft be feized of an eftate in *fee-fimple or fee-tail in* POSSESSION; and, therefore, a third mode is to put *the fee in remainder*; as to the hufband for life, with remainder to another perfon during the life of the hufband, with remainder to the hufband in fee or in tail. In this cafe, the intervening eftate to the other perfon prevents the remainder over from being executed in poffefsion in the hufband; and he is only feized in *pofsefsion* of the eftate for life.

So if the eftate be limited to the hufband and a ftranger for life, in joint tenancy,

nancy, with remainder to the hufband in
fee or in tail, the hufband fhall hold the
eftate for life in joint tenancy with the
ftranger, and the remainder will be only
executed *fub modo*, and not in poffefsion.
But this manner of limiting the eftate is
objectionable, as before noticed under the
firft mode, by reafon of the pofsibility of
the hufband furviving the ftranger,

The beft way is, therefore, to limit the
eftate *to fuch ufes as the hufband fhall ap-*
point, which gives him the power over the
whole fee; fo that he may pafs it to a
purchafer without any fine or concurrence
of the wife or others; and the purchafer,
on the execution of the power, fhall be *in*
from the original conveyance, and fo pa-
'ramount the claims of the wife; *and, in*
default of execution, to the husband for life,
with remainder to A. B. his executors and
adminiftrators, during the life of the huf-
band, which will put the limitation over
in tail or fee *in remainder*; and by limiting
the eftate to the *executors and adminiftrators*
of *A. B.* it will be more likely to prevent
the eftate falling into the hands of a minor,
in

But. n. (1.)
to *Co. Litt.*
379. b.
1 *Fearne.*509.

in cafe *A. B.* die before the hufband; and the eftate to *A. B.* being only an eftate *pour autre vie,* may (notwithftanding its being a *freehold*) with equal propriety be limited to *his executors and adminiftrators* as to his *heirs*, as they will not take by defcent, but as fpecial occupants.

See *ante.* ch. 4. p. 22.

A woman may alfo be precluded from claiming her dower in any lands of which the intended hufband fhall be feized during the coverture, by accepting a jointure according to the ftatute of Henry the Eighth. So fhe fhall be barred in equity by the acceptance of other confiderations, fuch as do not fall within that ftatute, as a yearly fum of money, though not charged on any fpecific fund.

Co. Litt. 36. a. & b. and Notes. 2 *Bl. Comm.* 137. 1 *Atk.* 563. Hervey *v.* Hervey. N. (1.) to *Co. Litt.* 36. b. & the books there referred to. Cafe of Drury *v.* Drury, 5 *Bro. Parl. Caf.* 570.

If there be any exifting term which was created before marriage, there fhall, in certain cafes, be a *ceffet executio* during the term.

Butl. n. 1. to *Co. Litt.* 208. a. & additional note.

CHAP. VII.

―――――――

OF AN ESTATE BY THE CURTESY.

AN eftate by the curtefy, like that in dower, arifes by act of law, and is an eftate *of freehold*; and, confequently, as it may be conveyed to a ftranger for the life of the tenant by the curtefy, it muft be conveyed by thofe means which the law appropriates for the transfer of freeholds, as by livery, or under the ftatute of Ufes.

2 Bl. Comm. 126. Litt. b. 1. c. 4. & Co. Litt. 29.a. to 30.b.

It may alfo be *furrendered* to the heir or reverfioner.

As an hufband fhall have his curtefy of a truft, the fame modes of prevention do not exift as exift with refpect to dower. But as he fhall not have his curtefy of a remainder or reverfion *on a freehold*, nor

of

of a freehold in poffefsion that is not a *fr. of inheritance,* the eftate by curtefy may be prevented by placing either the free-hold in poffefsion, or an intermediate eftate of freehold, or the inheritance, out of the wife.

CHAP. VIII.

OF AN ESTATE TAIL.

WHEN an eftate is limited to a perfon and *his defcendants*, it is called an *eftate tail*, as to a man *or* woman, or to a man *and* woman, and the heirs of *his*, *her*, or *their body or bodies*.

2 *Bl. Comm.* 110. *Litt.* b. 1. c. 2 *Wright's Ten.* 185. *Sulliv. Lect.* 121. *Watk.* No. lxxix. to *Gilb. Ten.* 418. & 1 *Watk. Cop.* ch. 4. p. 147. *Preft. on Eft.* 264.

If it be to a man *or* woman, and the heirs of his or her body, it is an eftate in tail *general*, as any heir of his or her body may inherit: but if it be to Thomas and the heirs of his body *by his wife Jane*, or to Jane and the heirs of her body *by her hufband Thomas*, or to Thomas *and* Jane and the heirs of *their bodies*, it is an eftate in *fpecial* tail; and fo alfo if it be to the heirs *male* of the body of A. B. As, in the firft cafe, no heirs of the body of Thomas can inherit but thofe who are born of Jane; nor, in the fecond, any heirs of the body

D   of

of Jane by any other hufband than Thomas; nor, in the third, any heir of the
body of Thomas who is not alfo heir of
the body of Jane, nor of Jane who is not
alfo the heir of the body of Thomas; or,
in other terms, no heir of the body of
Thomas by any other wife, nor of Jane
by any other hufband, fhall fucceed.

Hence if it be wifhed to fettle lands fo
that the entail may not be cut off by the
parents, it may fometimes be neceffary to
limit an eftate for life to one parent, and
the inheritance to the heirs of the body
of the other, as the entail would then be
in neither. The firft taking only for life,
and the other not taking at all; but the
heirs being in by purchafe. Or if the
eftate be the hufband's, to limit to him
for life, with remainder to the wife in
tail, as he being tenant for life only, cannot dock the entail, and the wife is prevented from doing fo by the ftatute of
Hen. 7. *c.* 20*.

---

* But as hufband and wife may *together* bar the entail, this is not always an effectual mode of prevention.

But

But as it is a rule, that " if the an- 1. *Co.* 104.
" ceftor, by any gift or conveyance, takes *Watk. Defc.* 157.
" an eftate of freehold, and in the fame 1. *Harg. Law Tr.* 485, 550.
" gift or conveyance an eftate is limited, *Preft. on the*
"· either mediately or immediately, to his *rule in Shel-lie's cafe.*
" or her heirs in fee or in tail, the words
"· *the heirs*" are words of limitation, and
" not words of purchafe," care muft be
taken, if it be intended that the entail
fhall not veft in the parents, to limit the
eftates fo as not to be capable of uniting;
as to the parent for *years*, as for ninety-nine
years if he fo long live, which will only
give him a *chattel intereft* that cannot
coalefce with the eftate limited to his
heirs, which is *a freehold*; or to give
an *equitable* eftate only to the parent, and
a *legal* one to the heirs; for eftates muft
be of the fame nature to be capable of
uniting, as both freehold, or both legal:
or to confine the particular eftate to *one*
parent, and limit the remainder to the
heirs of the body of *both*. And care
muft alfo be taken that *the whole of the
particular eftate be difpofed of*, leaft any
eftate of freehold be capable of *refulting*

to

to the anceſtor to whoſe heirs the eſtate is limited.

But the beſt and moſt uſual 'mode is to limit to the parent or parents for life', with remainder, not to the *heirs* of his, her, or their body or bodies, but to the *ſon* or *ſons* (or *children,*) and the heirs of his, her, or their body or bodies, ſo that the ſon, or ſons, or children,' ſhall take *as purchaſers*, as perſons *particularly and expreſsly deſignated*, and *not as the heir or heirs* of the parent or parents. But if the ſettlement be made *before* the birth · of ſuch children, the remainders limited to them muſt neceſſarily be *contingent ones* till they come *in eſſe*; and conſequently ſubject to deſtruction, or to being defeated by the parents; and hence the utility *of appointing truſtees for preſerving them.* The moſt common mode of limiting theſe remainders to the iſſue, is to *the firſt and other ſons*; but this mode is ſometimes objectionable, as it renders the eldeſt ſon independent on his parents; and it may, therefore, be adviſable to limit the eſtate *to ſuch ſon* of the marriage *as the parents,*

2. *Bl. Comm.* 171.
1. *Atk.* 581.
Hopkins *al.* Dare *v.* Hopkins.
Butl. add. n. to *Co. Litt.* 271. b. and n. (2) to 265, a. & 290. b. (*ſ.* 111.)
1. *Fearne.* (See index tit. 'Truſtees.)

3   *or*

or furvivor of them, fhall, by deed or will, *appoint,* and to the heirs of his body; and in default of fuch appointment, to the firft and other fons, &c. in the ufual manner.

An eftate tail cannot be transferred to another; but, as the tenant in tail has a fee (though reftricted) in him, he may convey a bafe fee to another, by leafe and releafe, bargain and fale enrolled, or by fine; that is, if he makes fuch convey-ance to A. and his heirs, A. and his heirs fhall have a fee fimple qualified, that is, fo long as the heirs of the tenant in tail continue. And if the tenant in tail have alfo the reverfion in himfelf, he may con-vey an abfolute fee to another, or gain an abfolute fee in himfelf, by levying a fine; for the fine paffes the reverfion, which is an abfolute fee, as well as the bafe fee; and when both fees are fixed in the fame perfon, the bafe fee merges in the abfo-lute one, fo that the abfolute, or rever-fionary fee comes into poffefsion.

No. 1. *to Co. Litt.* 331. a & the books there cited. Of *Difcon-tinuance,* fee *n.* (1.) *to Co. Litt.* 326, b. & (1) (2) to 327, a. 3. *Bl. Comm.* 171, 191. *Litt.* b. 3. c. 11. & *Co. Litt.* 325. *Gilb. Ten.* 107.

But

1. *Cru.* 274. But as the tenant in tail (while tenant in tail) *may charge the reverfion*, and as the fine when levied brings *the reverfion into poffefsion*, it is frequently prudent, 2. *Cru.* 284. and, indeed, neceffary, in order to gain a good title, to fuffer a recovery, as a fine lets in the charges of the tenant in tail, and a recovery gives a clear and new fee*.

2. *Bl. Comm.* 359. *Pigg.* 108. ch. 5. 2. *Cru.* 218. Hence then is a recovery fuffered by the tenant in tail, in moft cafes, the beft and moft effectual bar †; and this fhould be fuffered with (at leaft) *a double* voucher, for if fuffered with *a fingle one*, it only bars the eftate of which the tenant in tail is

---

* But a recovery will let in the charges of *the per-fon fuffering it,* though not thofe of his anceftors. See 2 *Cru.* 284, 8. & *poft.* B. 2. C. 16.

† In fome cafes indeed a fine is a more effectual bar than a recovery; as the former is declared an eftoppel or bar by the *Stat.* 32. *Hen.* 8. while it would be at leaft doubtful whether the iffue would be eftopped merely by the vouching of the anceftor, who had no eftate in the lands at the time to pafs. *Poft.* B. 2. C. 15. & C. 16.

actually

actually feized at the time; but if with a double or treble voucher it will bar every other intereft he may have in the premifes; as will appear under the head of RECOVERY.

A tenant in tail in poffefsion may alfo, in fome inftances, bar both his own iffue and thofe in remainder, by annexing a *warranty* to his grant, as the warranty will defcend to his heirs, and, if accompanied with affets, will bar his own iffue, and without affets will bar fuch of his heirs as may be in remainder or reverfion. But the propriety of this mode depends upon much nice matter, and fhould be had recourfe to with much caution ; for fhould *no affets actually defcend to the iffue*, they will not be barred, nor will the remainder-man or reverfioner, *unlefs he be alfo the heir of the warrantor*; for, unlefs he be *the heir* of the warrantor, he will not be fubject to the warranty.

See 2. *Burr.* 1072, &c.

a 2. *Bl. Comm.* 303.

Gilb. Ten. 133, & *Watk.* n. liv. &c. p. 400, &c.

The warranty defcending on the iffue is a *lineal* warranty, as the heir claims *through the warrantor*; and lineal warranty

is

is no bar without affets actually defcending. But the warranty defcending on thofe in remainder or reverfion is *collateral,* as they do *not claim through the warrantor, but immediately from the donor ;* and *collateral* warranty will bar without affets.

No. (1) to Co. Litt. 379. b. And fo eftablifhed is the power of the tenant in tail to deftroy the entail and alien by fine or recovery, that no condition reftrictive of fuch power is permitted to take effect.

And note, that exprefs power is given by ftatute to Commifsioners of Bankrupt to convey lands entailed of the Bankrupt, by bargain and fale enrolled.

CHAP. IX.

OF AN ESTATE IN FEE SIMPLE.

AN Eftate in fee fimple is either *abfo-* lute, or *qualified* or *bafe*. An eftate in fee *abfolute* is an eftate limited to a perfon and his heirs, general or indefinite. It is not confined to any particular line or fpecies of heirs, but is limited to the heirs generally; and it is the higheit eftate which the law acknowledges.

2. Bl. Comm. 104. *Litt.* b. 1. c. 1. *Wright*, *Ten.* 146. *Preff. Eff.* ch. 2.

An eftate in fee *qualified* or *bafe*, is an eftate to A. and his heirs *'till a certain event happen*, or *to be defeated if fuch an event occur :* as to A. and his heirs tenants of the manor of Dale. Here fo foon as A. or his heirs ceafe to be tenants of that manor the eftate will ceafe.

The eftate in fee fimple abfolute may be conveyed *ad infinitum*; but it being

an

an eftate of freehold in poffefsion (for we
are not here to fpeak of reverfions) the
freehold muft actually pafs; as by feoffment, leafe and releafe, bargain and fale
enrolled, &c.

An eftate in fee qualified or bafe may
alfo be transferred by the fame means,
fubject to the qualifications : but it cannot be conveyed difcharged of fuch qua-
lification, unlefs by wrong, as by a feoffment in fee abfolute, which would gain
a fee abfolute by difleifin*, and turn the
reverfion (if we may fo call it) to a
right, and which right would be barred
by a fine levied by the feoffee, unlefs the
perfon having fuch right claim within
the time allowed by the ftatute of
Hen. 8.

1. *Fearne,*
54⁵, ⁷.

A bafe or qualified fee may by pofsibility
continue for ever ; and the common law

---

* An eftate gained by wrong is always a *quafi*
fee : as the law cannot take notice of a wrong, it cannot of confequence fet any limits to that wrong. See
Ibb. 323.

does

does not permit any remainder to be limited on a fee either abfolute or bafe. A fee may, indeed, be limited on a fee by way of *executory devife*, or of *fhifting ufe* ; of which limitations we fhall fpeak in fubfequent chapters.

CHAP. X.

OF AN ESTATE IN PARCENARY.

2. Bl. Comm. 187, 323. *Litt.* b.3, c. 1, & the *Comment.* And fee *Comyns' Dig.* tit. Parceners, as to the general law on this fubject. * *Gilb. Ten.* 72—3. † *Touchft.* 14. 1 *Cru.* 104.

COPARENCERS always take by de-fcent; and, as they compofe but one heir, they have, as to fome purpofes, but one freehold; but, as to others, feveral; hence they may convey *to each other*, either by releafe, by feoffment*, or fine †.

As *to ftrangers*, they muft convey their refpective portions or fhares by the feveral modes of conveyance which pafs the freehold; as by fine, recovery, feoffment, leafe and releafe, or bargain and fale enrolled; or they may covenant to ftand feized.

Touchft. 291. But they cannot exchange with each other 'till partition.

If

If there be two parceners, and they make partition by confent, they may releafe to each other their refpective moieties, and there will be no necefsity for a leafe for a year (or bargain and fale), as the poffefsion at the time of partition would be in each.

CHAP. XI.

OF AN ESTATE IN JOINT-TENANCY.

2. Bl. Comm. JOINT-TENANTS always take *by pur-*
179.
Litt. b. 3. c. 3. *chafe*; and the proper and beft mode of
and the *Com-* creating an eftate in joint-tenancy is to
ment.
limit " to A. B. and C. D. and their af-
figns," if it be an eftate for life; or " to
A. B. and C. D. and their heirs," if in
But. (1) to fee. The limitation fometimes made
Co. Litt. 191, " to A. B. and C. D. and *the furvivors of*
a.
1 *Fearne,*283, *them, and the heirs of fuch furvivors,"* is
&c.
objectionable, as it has been fuppofed to
give *a contingent remainder to the furvivor*;
for, though the propriety of fuch a fup-
pofition may be queftionable, yet it would
be prudent to avoid the doubt.

But in the creation of a joint-tenancy
it is not only neceffary that the eftate to
the feveral perfons *be limited by the fame*
deed,

deed, but the estate in them must *vest at one* See *Co. Litt.*
and the same time; for if an estate be li- 188. a. & n.
mited to A. for life, with remainder to the *Fearne*, 460,
heirs of B. and C. (B. and C. being sup- 239, (3d ed.)
posed to be living,) and B. die *during the*
particular estate, when one moiety would
vest in *his* heirs, and afterwards C. die, *in*
the lifetime of A. when the other moiety
would vest in *his* heirs, the heirs of B.
and C. would take in common.

But if the estate be limited *by way of*
use it would be otherwise ; as the estate
would be in the truftee *till* the ufes arife ;
and *as* they arife the *cestui que use* shall be
in by the original feoffment or deed.

As joint-tenants are seized *per mie et* (a) 1*Vent.*78.
per tout they cannot *grant* (*a*), nor *bargain* *Cro.Jac.*696.
and fell (*a*), nor *furrender* (*b*), nor *devise* (*c*), (b) *Perk.* S.
to *each other*, nor can they *exchange* (*d*) 586, 7.
with each other, nor can one of them *enfeoff* (c) *Powell on*
his companion (*e*). (d) *Touchst.*
                                              292.
                                              (e) *Gilb. Ten.*
                                              73—4.

But each may fever the tenancy at his
pleafure by granting his portion over to a
ftranger, either to the ufe of fuch ftranger

                                         or

or in truſt for himſelf, by the uſual mode of conveying a freehold, or compel a partition, by ſtatute; or one may *releaſe to his companion.*

But joint-tenants may, either ſeverally or together, *exchange with a ſtranger,* or *ſurrender to the immediate reverſioner.*

CHAP. XII.

_____

OF A TENANCY IN COMMON.

TENANTS in common take alfo _by_ 2. _Bl. Comm._
purchafe, but hold by diftinct titles, and 191.
Litt. b. 3. c. 4.
have _feparate freeholds_, being not feized and the _Com._
per mie & per tout, as joint-tenants are : _ment._
and the beft way to create a tenancy in
common is either to limit one moiety of
the premifes exprefsly to one, and the
other moiety to the other, or to ufe the
words " to hold as tenants in common
and not as joint-tenants ;" as the law
may otherwife conftrue it a joint eftate.

As the poffefsion of tenants in common
is undivided 'till partition, they _cannot
exchange with each other_, though they _may_
exchange, either together or feparately,
with a ftranger.

But

Gilb. Ten. 74. But as the feifin of each is diftinct, and
their eftates feveral, one may *enfeoff* the
other; or, if the other have a greater
eftate, *furrender to him.* So one may *devife* his part to the other: but one cannot
releafe to his companion, as fuch.

Tenants in common may transfer their
refpective fhares *to ftrangers* by the ufual
modes of conveying freehold property;
and they may compel a partition among
themfelves.

CHAP. XIII.

_____

OF A REMAINDER.

A Remainder is that portion of interest 2 *Bl. Comm.* which, on the creation of a particular 164. 1 Fearne. eftate, *is limited over to another.*

Remainders are either *vefted* or *contin-* See 3. *Atk.* *tingent:* a *vefted* remainder is that *which* 138, &c. *is capable of being received in pofsefsion fhould the particular eftate happen to determine;* as to A. for life, remainder to B. and his heirs : here, as B. is in exiftence, he is capable (or his heirs if he die) of taking the poffefsion whenever A's death may occur.

A *contingent remainder* is when *the particular eftate may happen to determine before the perfon to whom the remainder is limited can take the pofsefsion;* as to A. for life,

with

with remainder to the right heirs of B.
Now, during B.'s life the remainder *is
contingent*, as he cannot have an heir till
his death ; and, therefore, fhould A. die
before B. there could be no one to take
the poffefsion.

In the creation of remainders the following rules muft be obferved :

1ft, There muft be a´ prefent, or particular, eftate created, which, if the remainder be a *vefted* one, muft be, at leaft,
for years; or, if the remainder be *contingent*, muft be an *eftate of freehold*, as a
freehold cannot commence *in futuro* by
the common law.

2dly, The particular eftate and the re_
mainders muft be created *by the fame
deed*.

3dly, The remainder muft veft in the
grantee, during the particular eftate, or
the very inftant it determines.

4thly,

4thly, And, if the remainder be contingent, it muft be limited to fome one
that may, by common pofsibility, or *po-*
tentia propinqua, be *in efse* at or before the
determination of the particular eftate.

2 *Hen.*
Blackft. 358.
Proctor v.
Bifhop of
Bath and
Wells, & al.

By the feudal law the freehold could
not be vacant, or, as it was termed, *in abcy-*
ance. There muft have been a tenant to
fulfil the feudal duties or returns, and
againft whom the rights of others might
be maintained.

If the tenancy once became vacant,
though but for an inftant, the lord was
warranted in entering on the lands, as
the confideration on the part of the tenant had ceafed ; and, confequently, as
no returns were made, there being no one
to render the fervices of the feud, the
lord was entitled to refume it. The tenant can only fubject his own eftate to
his own limitations ; and, therefore, the
moment that eftate ended, by the cef-
fion of the tenancy, all limitations of
that eftate were alfo at an end.

The

The lord on the efcheat is in paramount the tenant; he is in of an eftate from which the tenant's was originally derived.

Hence then the necefsity of an immediate eftate of freehold, or of a freehold in poffefsion, being vefted in fome perfon actually in exiftence who may fulfil the duties of the feud, and who may anfwer to the *præcipe* of ftrangers; and hence the necefsity alfo of the remainder taking effect during the exiftence of fuch particular eftate or *co infianti* that it determine; as a limitation of an eftate ' cannot take place when that eftate itfelf is no more.

Co. Litt. 270.
a. n. (3) 271.
b. n. (1).
Sand. on Ufes.
332, 455.

A *vefted* remainder may be conveyed to another by fine, by grant, by leafe and releafe, by bargain and fale enrolled; or the remainder-man may covenant to ftand feized. But it cannot be granted to commence *in*

See *Poft.* b. 2.
c. 1. of a
Feoffment.

futuro. And, as the freehold is in the particular tenant, a remainder cannot be the fubject of a *feoffment*; for a feoffment operates on the poffefsion which the remain-
der-

der-man has not to convey. For the fame See *Poft.* b. 2. reafon a *recovery* cannot be fuffered of a very. remainder, as the *præcipe* can only be brought againft *the tenant of the freehold in poffefsion.* But, if a *præcipe* be brought againft the tenant in poffefsion, and the remainder-man be vouched and enter into the warranty, he fhall be bound.

A *contingent* remainder may be barred ı *Fearne.*535, by *eftoppel* by matter of record, as a fine Sand. 335, or recovery ; and if the contingent re- mainder is fuch as to be defcendible to the heirs of the perfon to whom limited, if he die before the contingency happen, it may be *devifed,* or *paffed in equity:* but not otherwife.

Contingent remainders may be de- ftroyed, and prevented from taking effect, by deftroying the particular eftate by which they were fupported ; and, there- See *Ante.* fore, it is frequently neceffary to limit c. 8. p. 34. the legal eftate to truftees for the purpofe of preferving them.

If

1 *Fearne,* 49.
2 *J. Bl. Rep.*
687. Wills &
Palmer.
If it be intended in a fettlement to prevent the parent, from whom the lands
move, from defeating a remainder limited
to his heirs general or fpecial,—care muft
be taken that no particular eftate be
limited, or be capable of refulting, to fuch
parent ; as the eftates would, in fuch cafe,
unite, and the parent have an eftate in
fee or in tail in himfelf.

CHAP.

CHAP. XIV.

OF AN EXECUTORY DEVISE.

A N executory devife differs from a re- 2 *Bl. Comm.* 172. mainder (among other things) in this; that 2 *Fearne.* a remainder *muft have a particular eftate to fupport it*, while it is eſſential to an exe- cutory devife that *no particular eftate be* 2 *Saund. Rep.* *in exiftence*; it being a rule, that that 388. Purefoy *v.* Rogers. ſhall never be conftrued an executory devife which can be ſupported as a re- mainder.

By executory devife a fee or lefs eftate may be limited after a fee either abfolute or bafe.

Or a fee may be limited to commence *in futuro*; as, till fuch fee take effect, the inhe-

inheritance fhall defcend to the right heirs
of the teftator.

Remainders (or at leaft what we may
here call remainders) of chattels, either
real or perfonal, may be limited by executory devife, fo they be limited to a perfon or perfons in being, or to veft within
twenty-one years and a few months after
the death of a perfon or perfons in being;
but if the remainder be fuch as, if it were
of freehold property, would amount to an
exprefs entail, it fhall reft in the perfon in
whom it fo vefts, and be at fuch perfon's
difpofal, or to go to his reprefentative on
his death.

An executory devife cannot be barred
or deftroyed by any act *of the perfon taking
the preceding fee*, though by feoffment or
matter of record.

But *the perfon entitled to the executory
eftate* may bar his own claim by *releafe to the
firft taker in pofsefsion*; or *afsign it in equity*
3   *for*

for a valuable confideration; or *devife it by his laft will.*

So if *the perfon entitled to the executory eftate comes in as a vouchee on a common recovery*; fo *if he levy a fine*, it fhall bar him by eftoppel.

CHAP.

CHAP. XV.

OF A CONDITIONAL LIMITATION.

1 *Fearne.* 9.
414.
Sand. Uses.
182. &c.

A *Remainder* is to *commence* when *the particular estate* is, from its very nature, to *determine*; it is, as it were, a continuance of *the same estate; it is a part of the same whole.* *A conditional limitation* is *not* a *continuance of the estate first limited,* but is entirely a *different* and *separate* estate. It is *not* to commence *on the determination of the first, but the first is to determine when the latter commences.* It is *the commencement of the latter* which refcinds and deftroys the former; and not the *ceafing of the former* which gives exiftence to the laft. The particular eftate and remainders are, in fact, as the very terms imply, *but one and the same eftate.* The eftate firft appointed, and the conditional limitations, are *feparate* and *diftinct eftates.*

If

If *an estate tail* is first limited, and then a conditional limitation is made upon that estate, *a recovery* suffered by the tenant in tail, before the event or condition happen on which the limitation is to arise, will bar the estate depending on that event or condition.

But this is properly a *remainder.* See 2 *Fearne.* 52. &c.

As to the barring such conditional limitation by *estoppel*, and assigning in equity, or devising it, the law seems to be the same as with respect to an executory devise.

CHAP.

CHAP. XVI.

OF A REVERSION.

2 Bl. Comm. 175. Co.Litt. 22.b. Plowd. 151. Throckmorton v. Tracy. WHEN a perfon has an intereft in lands, and grants *a portion of that intereft,* or, in other terms, *a lefs eftate than he has in himfelf,* the poffefsion of thofe lands fhall, on the determination of the granted intereft or eftate, *return* or *revert to the grantor.*

It muft here be remarked, that it is faid the *pofsefsion* of the lands fhall return to the grantor on the determination of the grant, for a *prefent intereft* remains even during the exiftence of the grant in the perfon making it; and this intereft is that which is called *his reverfion,* or, more properly, *his right of reverter.*

This

This right of reverter can only arife by
the *act of law*; it *cannot be created by the
act of the party*, though it is a confequence
of his previous act. If a perfon limit particular eftates to ftrangers with the ultimate limitation to himfelf in fee, or to his
own right heirs, the latter limitation fhall
not take effect *as a remainder*, or by reafon *Watk. on Defc.*
of the *exprefs limitation* of the grantor; but, 168.
as the law would have given to him or his
heirs, as a confequence of the preceding
limitation, the fame intereft or eftate as
the exprefs words would have conveyed,
thofe words fhall be deemed wholly nugatory, and the grantor or his heirs fhall be
in *in reverfion*, or of *the old eftate.*

A reverfion, being *an immediate intereft,* *Watk. on Defc.*
may be conveyed to another perfon, though 110. 111.
to an utter ftranger. The conveyance of
it need not be confined, like the conveyance of a right, to the actual tenant of the
freehold. The proper mode of conveying a reverfion is by *grant**; though it

* Mr. *Fearne* is reprefented as having been of opinion (*Pofthum. Works*, 28.) that the *grant* of a reverfion,

* See n. (1.) may alſo be paſſed by *a leaſe and releaſe* *,
to *Co. Litt.*
270. a. & or *bargain and ſale*, ſuch bargain and ſale
n. (1.) to 271.
b. ſ. iii. being regularly enrolled; or the reverſioner
Sand. Uſes.
450—5. 469.

---

verſion, in conſideration of *money*, *would require en-rollment under the ſtatute of Henry* VIII. But he was evidently miſtaken if he entertained ſuch opinion, as the ſtatute of 27 *Hen.* VIII. *c.* 16. is exprefsly con-fined to conveyance by bargain and ſale *only*, and does not embrace grants, which have nothing to do with a bargain and ſale. Beſides, that ſtatute has an imme-diate and manifeſt relation to *the ſtatute of uſes*; and was ordained in order to prevent *ſecret transfers*, which might have been effeſted by a bargain and ſale, as the bargainor would ſtand ſeized to an uſe, and that uſe would have been immediately executed by the ſtatute, as, at this time, is the caſe of a bargain and ſale of a chattel intereſt, or leaſe for a year. The *bargain and ſale* were, therefore, ordered to be enrolled; but *a grant* of a reverſion was *not*, at the time of that ſtatute, a *ſecret conveyance*, as it was not good without

Of *attornment*, *attornment*, which was a matter of publicity, and an-See *Gilb. Ten.*
81. & *poſt.* ſwered the ſame purpoſes as livery did on a feoff-
b. 2. c. 2. ment.

2 *Vent.* 149. And the only caſe which Mr. *Fearne* has referred to
&c. .is that of *Lade v.* Baker, which cannot apply to the ſub-ject at this day, ſince the ſtatute of *Ann* has rendered attornment unneceſſary.

may

may *covenant to ftand feized* †; but a re- † 2 *Co.* 15.
verfion cannot be granted to commence *in* cafe.
futuro ‡.

‡ *Watk. of*
Defc. 111.
n. (t.)

But, even anterially to the ftatute of
frauds (29 *Car.* II.), a reverfion could not
be conveyed *by parol*; it muft have been
by deed, as it lay not in livery. For where
the pofsefsion did not pafs, the law required
a deed, or a folemn inftrument under feal,
when there was no matter of record, as the
evidence of the transfer.

A reverfion may alfo be *charged* by the
perfon entitled to it.

If an eftate tail be created, the reverfion, See *ante. c.* 8.
unlefs it be in the crown, may be barred c. 16.
or deftroyed by the tenant in tail fuffering
a recovery of the premifes by virtue of the
ftatutes of *Hen.* VII. & VIII.

& *poft.* b. 2.

The reverfioner continues tenant to the
lord during the exiftence of the particular
eftate; and the particular grantee fhall
hold of the reverfioner; and, as a neceffary

F   confe-

confequence or incident, the rent, fealty, &c. fhall always follow the reverfion.

Plowd. 153. 155.

As the creation of a particular eftate is of abfolute necefsity to give exiftence to a reverfion, fo the continuance of the reverfion depends upon the continuance of the particular eftate; for if, by any means, as by forfeiture, furrender, or regular expiration, fuch particular eftate determine, the intereft of the grantor ceafes, of necefsity, to be an eftate *in reverfion*, and becomes an eftate *in pofsefsion*, and into which he may immediately enter.

CHAP XVII.

OF A RIGHT.

O NE perfon may have *the actual pof-* *fefsion* of certain lands, and another the *right of pofsefsion,* or the *right of propriety*; as, if a perfon enter wrongfully into my lands, he will have the *actual* poffefsion; but I may enter and ouft him if I pleafe, as the *right of pofsefsion* is in me. If, however, I do not exert that right, and enter within a limited time, my power of entering is taken away, and I am driven *to my action* to recover the poffefsion; and if I do not avail myfelf of my poffeffory action, I fhall have only *a right of propriety,* or *mere right,* left.

Gilb.Ten. 21. &c. 37. &c.
2 Bl. Comm. 195.

A *right* is *not grantable* * *over*; it can only be *extinguifhed.* It cannot be even *furrendered* †; nor will it pafs to a *ftranger* by

* 10 *Co.* 46. b. Lampett's cafe. n.(1.) to *Co. Litt.* 265. a.
† *Co. Litt.* 338. a.

* *Touchft.* 14.
2 *Co.* 55. 56.
Buckler's
cafe.
by *fine**, though by fuch fine the right would be *barred*, as the cognizor cannot claim a right ¡againſt his own fine, which is a matter of record, and, by confequence, an eftoppel; as by that fine he *has acknowledged the right to be in another.*

Plowd. 485.
It is not *devifable*. The proper mode of extinguifhment is that of *a releafe*, or fine *fur cognizance de droit tantum*, to the perſon in actual poffefsion of the lands.

CHAP. XVIII.

OF A POSSIBILITY.

A Pofsibility cannot be on a pofsibi- *(a)* 4 *Co.* 50 b.
lity *(a)*. A pofsibility may be *releafed (b)*; ^{*(b)* 1 *Strange.*} 132. 2 *Atk.*
is *devifable (c)*; is *afsignable by commifsioners* ^{420.} *(c)* 1 *Hen.*
of bankrupt (d). It may be barred *by fine,* ^{*Blackft.* 30.}
by way of eftoppel *(e)*; but it fhould feem *Eaft* 88.
not otherwife *(f)*. So it *is afsignable in* ^{*(a)* 2 *Pr.Wms.*} 132. 2 *Atk.*
equity, at leaft if accompanied with an in- ^{420.} *(e)* 10 *Co.*
tereft *(g)*; fo an agreement to fettle lands 50. a.
in pofsibility fhall be decreed, if they 390. ^{*(f)* See 1 *Ves.*}
afterwards defcend *(h)*. ^{*(g)* 2 *Fearne,*}
522. 2 *Bl.*
Comm. 290.
(h) 1 *Ch.Rep.*
158.

CHAP.

CHAP. XIX.

OF AN EQUITY OF REDEMPTION.

2. *Bl. Comm.* 158.
Powell on Mortg. paſſim.
*Butl.*n.(1.) to
Co. Litt. 205.
a. & (1.) to
208. a.

IF a perſon convey lands to another on condition, as á ſecurity for money, and the condition be broken, he may, under certain circumſtances, *redeem* the premiſes; and this privilege is denominated his *equity of redemption.*

Such equity of redemption may be *re-leaſed* to the perſon in poſſeſsion. Some-times, indeed, the conveyance called *a leaſe and releaſe* is adopted; but then the latter ſpecies of conveyance does not ope-rate as a leaſe and releaſe with reſpect to the equity, as a perſon *cannot be ſeized of an equity to an uſe*; and, conſequently, as no uſe ariſes by the bargain and ſale, the releaſe can only operate, with reſpect to

4   the

the equity, as a mere or proper releafe; juft as it would have done *without* fuch a bargain and fale, or leafe for a year.

The conveyance by leafe and releafe is, therefore, adopted for caution only; as, *in cafe there be an equity* only in the perfon intending to convey, fuch releafe will operate *as a common releafe*, and fo pafs it, notwithftanding the bargain and fale; and, *in cafe there be any legal freehold, intereft, or eftate, left in the mortgagor*, by reafon of any defect in the mortgage deeds, *then* the bargain and fale will operate on fuch legal intereft or eftate, and, with the releafe, pafs that alfo.

In like manner, as a court of equity confiders a mortgage, though in fee, merely *as a fecurity for money* till the time of redemption be paft, the mortgagor frequently difpofes of his own equity, or right of redemption, to another. This can properly be only by way of *afsignment, grant,* or *devife*; for he *cannot* pafs it by *feoffment, bargain and fale,* nor, confe

See 3 *Bro.Ch. Ca.* 289. Trafh *v.* White.

F 4 quently,

quently, by *leafe and releafe*, as the feifin, or legal eftate, *is in the mortgagee*; though the leafe and releafe are often adopted for the reafon before noticed with refpect to the conveyance of fuch an equity to the perfon in poffefsion.

CHAP.

CHAP. XX.

OF USES AND TRUSTS.

It is neceſſary to the creation of ſuch an ufe as may be executed by the ſtatute, that there be a *perſon to ſtand ſeized of certain hereditaments to ſuch an uſe*; that there be *a perſon capable of taking that uſe*; and that there be *privity of eſtate* and *privity of perſon.* *2 Bl. Comm. 327. Butl.n.(1.)to Co. Litt. 271. b.(1.) to 290. b. 384. a. & add. notes. Booth's Opin. at the end of Touchſt. & in 1 Coll. Jurid. 421. Sand. Uſes. paſſim.*

1ſt, There muſt be a *perſon ſeized*; for a *corporation* cannot ſtand ſeized to an ufe; and, therefore, if a corporation convey, it muſt be by feoffment, leafe (with an actual entry) and releaſe, &c. though the courts *Sand. 446.* will, if poſſible, ſupport a bargain and fale by a corporation, as ſome other ſpecies of conveyance, rather than that it ſhould avoid its own act.

2dly, There

2dly, There muſt be a perſon *ſeized* of *hereditaments*; for *chattels,* whether real or perſonal, are not within the ſtatute: though a perſon may ſtand ſeized of the freehold to the uſe of another for a chattel intereſt; as *A. B.* being ſeized in fee, may covenant to ſtand ſeized to the uſe of *C. D. for years;* and ſuch uſe will be executed by the ſtatute. And this is every day ſeen by the leaſe, or, more properly, by the bargain and ſale, upon which a releaſe is grounded. But chattel intereſts may be conveyed ſubject to certain *truſts,* as commonly practiſed.

3dly, There muſt be a perſon *capable of receiving the uſe*; and, therefore, a limitation to the uſe of a corporation would not be good without licence, as it would be within the ſtatutes of Mortmain.

4thly, There muſt be *privity of eſtate*; for he who comes in in the *poſt,* or paramount the perſon limiting, ſhall not be ſubject to it.

5thly, There

5thly, There muſt be a *privity of per-* 1 *Fearne*,479.
ſon; for a purchaſer *without notice* ſhall
not hold charged.

There cannot be *an uſe upon an uſe.* If
an eſtate be limited to *A. B.* and his heirs,
to the uſe of *C. D.* and his heirs, to the uſe
of *E. F.* and his heirs, the ſtatute ſhall
execute *only the firſt uſe*, or that to *C. D.*
and the limitation to *E. F.* will be only *a*
truſt in equity *.

Upon

---

* If the limitation to *E. F.* and his heirs be intended as *a truſt*, it would be prudent to give the eſtate
to *A. B.* and his heirs, to the uſe of *C. D.* and his
heirs, to the uſe of, or in truſt for, *E. F.* and his heirs;
for if it be given to *A. B.* and his heirs, *to the uſe of*
himſelf (A. B.) *and his heirs*, to the uſe of, or in truſt
for, *E. F.* and his heirs, it might be open to the objection, that *A. B.* would be *in by the common law*;
and ſo the limitation of the uſe *to him and his heirs* be
nugatory; and that, conſequently, the limitation to
E. F. would, in ſuch caſe, be, in fact, *the firſt uſe*, and
executable by the ſtatute; and, conſequently, that
E. F. would take *the legal eſtate* to him and his heirs.—
Now, whether ſuch objection could be ſupported or
not, it would be highly proper to obviate it by limiting the eſtate to *A. B.* (an indifferent perſon) and his
heirs,

2 *Bl. Comm.*
336.

Upon this principle, however abfurd in itfelf, many important doctrines are founded. Hence, if it be wifhed that a perfon fhall have only *a truſt eſtate*, care fhould be taken to limit a preceding, and at leaſt commenfurate, ufe, fo as to be executed by the ſtatute; as, " to *A. B.* and his heirs, *to the uſe of him and his heirs during the life of* C. D. and from and after the deceafe of the faid *C. D. to the uſe of the heirs of the body of the faid C. D. ;*" when the eſtate limited to *C. D.* would *be a truſt only*; and the remainder to the heirs of his body would be a proper ufe, executed by the ſtatute the moment he died. And the eſtate to him being equitable, and that to his heirs legal, could not unite; and fo the latter would not be barrable by him.

---

heirs, *to the uſe of* C. D. AND E. F. (the truſtees) *and their heirs*, to the ufe of, or rather in truſt for, *G. H.* and his heirs, as then the ufe to the truſtees would be executed, and the legal eſtate would, unqueſtionably, be in fuch truſtees; and, confequently, any fubfequent limitations would be inexecutable by the ſtatute.

Hence

Hence alfo an ufe cannot be limited on
a *bargain and fale* to any but the *bargainee*;
for, till enrollment,the bargainee himfelf has
but an ufe, and he cannot be feized of an ufe
to the ufe of another perfon; and the limitation over would be a truft: and fo as to a
covenant to ftand feized. If, therefore, it be
intended that a third perfon fhould take an
ufe executable by the ftatute, fome other
fpecies of conveyance (as a *fine*, *feoffment*,
or *leafe and releafe*) fhould be had recourfe
to.

An ufe need not take effect immediately
on the creation of the deed, like an eftate
of freehold. It may commence in *futuro*;
for the freehold remains in the truftee, or
covenantor, or bargainor, who is to anfwer to the *præcipe* of others, and perform
the feudal duties. But the contingency
upon which the ufe is to arife muft be fuch
as may happen within a reafonable period,
as a life or lives in being, or 21 years
afterwards; and ufes fo limited are called
contingent or *fpringing ufes*, which may be 1 *Fearne*,435,
deftroyed or defeated *by deftroying the eftate* $^{436.}$
out of which they are to fpring.

An

See as to
ſhifting the
ſecond eſtate
on the acceſ-
ſion to the
family eſtate,
Butl. n. to *Co.*
Litt. 327. b.
328.

An uſe may alſo be limited ſo as *to change, after execution, to another perſon;* as to the uſe of *B.* for life, remainder to firſt and other ſons in tail, remainder in fee; *provided that if there be no iſſue living at the death of B.* then to the right heirs of *C.* for ever. And this is called a *ſhifting* or *ſecondary* uſe; but, like the latter, it muſt take effect, if at all, within a life or lives in being, &c.

If ſuch ſhifting uſe be limited on an eſtate *in fee,* it *cannot be deſtroyed or barred by the previous taker;* but, if on a limitation *in tail,* it may.

1 *Fearne*, 205. And ſo with reſpect to *truſts:* ſome are completely eſtabliſhed, and ſo as to take effect immediately, by the very deed which conveys the legal eſtate to the truſtee, and are, therefore, frequently called truſts *executed;* while others are to be carried into execution by ſome future act to be done by the truſtee; and theſe are often denominated truſts *executory.* The *firſt* ſpecies of truſts *have the ſame con-ſtruction as legal eſtates;* while the *latter*

are

are *carried into execution fo as beft to anfwer the intention of the perfon creating them.*

When an ufe is wholly or partially un-difpofed of, it fhall *refult* to the grantor.

The *ceftui que truft* may transfer his inte- *Piggot,* 184.
reft over to a ftranger; and if fuch *ceftui que* 214.
truft be tenant in tail in poffefsion, he 120.
may even fuffer *a common recovery*, though 1 *Cru.* 187.
there be no legal tenant to the *præcipe*;
fo he may levy *a fine.*

Piggot, 184.
1 *Coll. Jurid.*
214.
2 *Ves. Jun.*
120.
1 *Cru.* 187.

In certain cafes the *ceftui que truft* may 1 *Fearne,*483.
call in the legal eftate; and, by a bill in *Sand.* 261.
equity, oblige the truftees to convey.

In fome cafes it is proper to keep the legal eftate outftanding, in order to guard againft mefne incumbrances, &c. This is ufual with refpect to terms of years, which fhould, generally, be kept on foot for the fecurity of the purchafer, and, in fuch cafes, carefully afsigned to a perfon of his own nomination in truft to attend the freehold or inheritance.

If

Watk. on Defc.
191.
2 *Ves. Jun.*
120. Brydges
v. Brydges.
If a truft and legal eftate unite in the fame perfon, the former, generally fpeaking, becomes merged or extinguifhed.

In conveyances creating trufts there fhould be claufes enabling the truftees to deduct expences; and fometimes an exprefs allowance fhould be given them for their time and trouble; that they fhall not be anfwerable for monies not actually received by them, or for what fhall be loft without their fault. It is frequently neceffary alfo to give them power, either with or without confent, to fell or exchange the lands, or transfer ftock, &c.

CHAP.

CHAP. XXI.

─────────────

OF POWERS.

A POWER is an authority exprefsly re- *Butl.* n. (1.)
ferved to the grantor, or exprefsly given to *Co. Litt.* 342.b. & *add.*
to another, to be exercifed over lands, &c. n. to 271. *Booth's Opin.*
granted or conveyed at the time of the at the end of *Touchft.* & 1
creation of fuch power. *Coll. Jurid.* 421.
Powell on Powers.

Powers are either *collateral* or *relating to* 2 *Fearne*, 334,
the land; and thofe *relating to the land* are &c. *in note.*
either *appendant* (or *annexed to the eftate*) *Sand. Ufes.* 288, 303,
or in *grofs.* 531—555.

Collateral powers are thofe which are given to *ftrangers*; that is, *to perfons who have neither a prefent nor future eftate or intereft in the lands.*

Powers

Powers *relating to the land* are thofe referved or given to pefons who *have either a
prefent or future eftate or intereft in the lands.*
Thofe *appendant, or annexed to the eftate,*
are where a perfon· has an eftate in the
land, and the eftate to be created by the
power is to take effect in poffefsion *during
the continuance of the eftate to which the
power is annexed*; as to make leafes. ˋ

Thofe in *grofs* are where the perfon **to**
whom they are given has an eftate in the
land, but the eftate to be created under,
or by virtue of, the power, is not to take
effect *till after the determination of the eftate
to which it relates*; as to jointure an after-
taken wife.

Great care fhould be taken in the creation of powers, as the appointer can only
act according to the authority given. If
power be given *to hufband and wife,* the
furvivor cannot appoint; and, therefore, if
it be intended that the furvivor fhould appoint, fuch power fhould be exprefsly given
" *to the furvivor of them.*" If a power be
given

given to *A.B.* to appoint by *deed*, he cannot appoint *by will*; and, therefore, if it be meaned that he *fhould* appoint by will, it fhould be fo faid.

· If the power be fimply to defignate a perfon, or the like, it 'fhould not be clog-ged with many ceremonies; but, if col-lufion or influence is feared, it would be proper to throw certain ceremonies in the way; as to require three or four witneffes, " *not being menial fervants*," or the like.

· Again; it fhould be confidered whether the eftates to be taken under the power, when executed, are to be eftates *in pof-feſsion*, or mere *trufts:* if the *former*, the eftates fhould be conveyed by the deed creating fuch power to the truftees and their heirs, *to fuch ufes as A. B. fhall ap-point*; and then, on the appointment, *the ftatute will execute the ufe*; if the *latter*, *the legal eftate fhould be placed in the truſtees*; as to *A.* and his heirs, *to the ufe of B. and C.* (the truftees) *and their heirs*, to and upon fuch trufts, and for fuch eftate or eftates, ends, intents, and purpofes, as *D.*

fhall

ſhall appoint, as the uſe would then be *executed in the truſtees*, and the eſtates taken under the appointment would be *truſt eſtates* only.

By a power to appoint to *children*, the appointer cannot give an eſtate to *grand-children*. If the grand-children are to take therefore, it ſhould be provided for: That, in caſe *any* or *all* of the ſaid children die before the power be executed, leaving lawful iſſue, then to appoint among the children then living, and the iſſue of ſuch children who ſhall then be dead, in ſuch ſhares, &c.

So if *the appointer* die before execution, the power, as to *diſcretion*, ſhall ceaſe; and, therefore, in ſome inſtances, it may be prudent to provide for that event: as, in caſe the ſaid *A. B.* ſhall happen to die in the life-time of *C. D.* or before there be iſſue of *E. F.* &c. without making any appointment, or only a partial or defective appointment, then the like power as given to the ſaid *A. B.* ſhall be veſted in *G. H.* &c. Though when an execution is pre-

2 *Ves.* 640.
Alexander *v.* Alexander.

See 2 *Ves. Jun.* 357.
Routledge *v.* Dorril.

prevented by death, which is an act of God, a court of equity will aid, if it be not merely dependent *upon perfonal difcretion.*

So it is often proper to make the power more general than is fometimes done: as to fuch ufes, and for fuch eftates, &c. as *A. B.* fhall *from time to time* appoint, &c. as *A. B.* may then execute his power *at different times,* and over *different parts of the lands.* Powell, 263, 341.

So provifion fhould be made in cafe of *no appointment,* or of a *defective* or *partial appointment:* as, and in default of fuch appointment, then as to fuch part or parts of the faid premifes, or to fuch portion or portions of intereft of and in the fame, to which fuch appointment fhall not extend, to the ufe, &c.

So if it be intended that *A. B.* fhould revoke his appointment, and re-appoint, power fhould be exprefsly given him, *from time to time, either wholly or partially, to revoke fuch appointment, and limit new ufes.*

In

In the *execution* of a power it is moftly proper *to recite it,* and always to *make it apparent on the face of the inftrument that it is the appointer's intention to execute and act under the power*; and, therefore, reference fhould be made to the premifes by defcription, &c. And it is beft to fay exprefsly, that *under and by virtue of fuch power, fo given, &c. and in execution of it, the faid A. B. doth appoint, &c.*

Too great care cannot pofsibly be taken in the execution, to comply with and follow the requifite ceremonies: as, if it be given to *C. D.* to appoint, with the approbation of her hufband, teftified by his being party to and executing the deed in the prefence of three witneffes, &c. *the approbation of the hufband, his being a party, his executing the deed in the prefence of three witneffes,* &c. muft be fcrupuloufly complied with, and may be even ftated.

And as the *excefs* only, in the execution of an appointment, will be bad, and a deficient execution cannot be extended, it is prudent *to be very full in the execution,*

as

as the furplufage fhall not vitiate what
would otherwife be good.

If power of revocation and re-appoint-
ment be given, and the appointer execute,
he fhould referve in fuch appointment a *new
power of revocation, with power alfo to appoint
new ufes*; as, without this exprefs refervation
of future revocation and new appointment, the firft may often be abfolute.

2 *Burr.* 1148.
Preced.Chanc.
474.
Touchft. 524.
& *Booth's*
Opin. ibid.
& 1 *Cell.*
Jurid.

Powers *appendant* may be *deftroyed* by
leafe and releafe, bargain and fale, feoffment, fine, or recovery; thofe *in grofs*
by the three latter fpecies of conveyance, or they may be releafed. Powers
collateral cannot be deftroyed by the act
of the perfon to whom they are given.

Butl. n. (1.)
to *Co. Litt.*
271. b. f. iv.

And note, as the appointer is merely an
inftrument, the appointee fhall be in by
the original deed.

2 *Ves.* 78.
Co. Litt.
299. b. n.(1.)
1 *Fearne*, 99,
&c.
2 *Burr.* 879.

CHAP.

CHAP. XXII.

OF RENTS.

2. Bl. Comm. 41. *Gilb. on Rents.* A Rent *(Reditus)* is, properly, a fum of money, or other thing, to be rendered periodically, in confequence of an exprefs refervation in a grant or demife of lands or tenements, the reverfion of which is in the grantor or perfon demifing.

A rent, therefore, neceffarily fuppofes a reception of fuch lands or tenements from another, to whom they primarily belonged, and in whom the ultimate property is ftill vefted : hence it follows, that, if lands or tenements were *not* de-rived from another, as anciently when lands were held *in allodio*, or if no other perfon has fuch ultimate property in him, there can be no rent.

If

If a perfon, confequently grants over *his whole property* in certain premifes to another, the other, (or grantee) paying to fuch perfon and his heirs a certain fum annually for ever, fuch annual fum will *not be properly a rent*, as the grantor has no ultimate property or reverfion in him. Such annual payment is, indeed, commonly denominated a *rent* charge or *rent* feck ; but it is not ftrictly and in reality a *rent* ; and the law accordingly refpected it differently, as it gave the grantor no power of diftrefs without a fpecial ftipulation.

Again, if a perfon grants an annual fum to be iffuing out of his lands to another and his heirs for ever, without parting with any property in the lands themfelves, it will be no *rent*, as it is no *return*, no *compenfation*, fince the grantee has no lands in confequence of fuch grant for which to *render* or *return* a *compenfation*.

As, however, the fum ftipulated to be paid is an annual, or, at leaft, a periodical fum, and

and to be iffuing out of lands, it is, by reafon of its analogy to the proper rent, denominated a *rent* charge, or a *rent* feck, according as the power of diftrefs was or was not given.

Again, as a proper rent is a compenfation or return for the enjoyment of a particular eftate, it follows that when the particular eftate determine the rent muft alfo ceafe.

As the returns of the feud were conditions, on the breach of which the feud reverted to the lord, fo the non-payment of rent occafioned a forfeiture of the lands out of which it was to iffue.

The rigour of the feudal law with refpect to forfeiture, in the cafes of non-payment of rent, was foon, however, abated. It was thought unreafonably fevere to infift on an abfolute forfeiture of the premifes on non-payment of rent at the very day on which it was referved ; and the law of diftreffes was, therefore, adopted from the civil code. But, as the

5   diftrefs

diftrefs was merely a fubftitute for the feudal forfeiture, it follows that it could only take place where *that* was allowed. If a perfon had no right of reverter, there-fore, as in the cafes where the lands out of which the annual payment was to iffue had not moved from him, or where he had parted with his ultimate property in the lands which had originally moved from him, there could be no forfeiture to him of the lands or tenements ; and con-fequently he could not be entitled to a diftrefs which was merely fubftituted for the former remedy. If the particular eftate for which the rent was to be ren-dered had expired, there could pofsibly be no forfeiture ; as the eftate which only could have been the fubject of forfeiture had ceafed to exift ; and, confequently, there could be no diftrefs.

In the two former cafes, indeed, a power of diftrefs might have been exprefsly created, but then it was, as the terms import, a private ftipulation between the particular parties, and not a remedy given by the law. The law, however, has been altered

in

this refpect, by ftatute 4 *Geo.* 2. c. 28 ; and in the cafe of the expiration of the term by the ftatute 8 *Anne, c.* 14.

If the leffor be feized *in fee fimple*, the proper rent fhould be referved *to him*, " *his heirs and afsigns ;*" if he have only a *chattel interefi*, to *him*, " *his executors, ad-miniftrators, and afsigns.*" Though the beft way of referving fuch rent is to re-ferve it *generally*, without exprefsing to whom ; as " yielding and paying there-fore, yearly, during the faid term, the fum of, &c." as the law will give it to the perfon who fhall be, from time to time, entitled to the immediate reverfion, which the rent will always follow ; for as the rent is only a compenfation for the lands, it fhall go to him who would have been entitled to the lands in cafe the compenfation failed.

8 *Co.* 71. a.
1. *Vent.* 148.
161.
Gilb. Rents,
64, &c.

Though the ftatute, 4 *Geo.* 2. has given the fame power of diftrefs in cafes of rents feck as in thofe of rent charge, it is ftill ufual to infert a fpecial power of diftrefs in the grants of rent ; and fuch
fpecial

ſpecial power is generally accompanied alſo with a clauſe of entry on non-payment, with power to enjoy till the arrears be ſatisfied.

Rents charge or ſeck may be created *Sand.* 332. by *fine**, *recovery, bargain and ſale, leaſe and releaſe, covenant to ſtand ſeized,* or *grant;* and may be limited to one in tail with remainders over.

They may alſo be *releaſed to the perſon* *Sand.* 163. *ſeized of the lands;* or *conveyed to a ſtranger* $\begin{smallmatrix}Butl. \text{ n. } (2)\\to \text{ } Co. \text{ } Litt.\end{smallmatrix}$ by *grant,* and that even to commence *in* 298. a. *futuro,* or *under the ſtatute of uſes;* as a perſon may be ſeized of a rent to an uſe, which uſe will be immediately executed *Pigg.* 97. by the ſtatute. So a *fine* or *recovery* may $\begin{smallmatrix}1. \text{ } Cru. \text{ } 120,\\248. \text{ } 2. \text{ } ibid.\end{smallmatrix}$ be of a rent. 215.

If a Rent be limited to A. B. in tail *with* *Pigg.* 97. *remainder over in fee,* A. by ſuffering a $\begin{smallmatrix}Butl. \text{ n. } (2)\\to \text{ } Co. \text{ } Litt.\end{smallmatrix}$ recovery, may bar his iſſue and the 298. a. remainder over, and gain *a clear and*

---

* But not by a fine *executed.* See 1. *Cru.* 62.

abſolute

abſolute fee in it : But if a rent be granted *de novo* to A. in tail *without a remainder over,* and A. ſuffer a recovery, he ſhall only acquire *a baſe fee determinable on failure of his iſſue.*

PRINCIPLES

OF

CONVEYANCING, &c.

BOOK II.

OF CONVEYANCES AS THEY RELATE TO ESTATES.

CHAP. I.

OF A FEOFFMENT.

A Feoffment is a conveyance which operates by *tranfmutation of poffefsion* : it is effential to its completion that the *feifin** be paffed. Hence it can only be adopted in cafes where the feifin may be, and is actually to be, conveyed ; as in the transfer of eftates of *freehold in poffefsion*. In the transfer of *chattel interefts* there is no feifin to be conveyed, as the feifin remains

2. *Bl. Comm.* 310. *Touchft.* 203. *But. n.* (1) to *Co. Litt.* 271, b *Sand. Ufes,* 258.

* Of Livery. See *Watk.* N. xxix. to *Gilb. Ten.*

in

in the freeholder: hence a term of years cannot be conveyed by feoffment. In the transfer of *reverſions* or *remainders* on a freehold, the actual or corporal feiſin is not concerned, as it continues in the particular tenants: Hence they cannot paſs by feoffment, but by *grant*. So of *equitable intereſts*, &c.

Hence, too, feoffments can only be made by a perſon *in the actual feiſin* to a perſon who is *not in the actual feiſin:* and, therefore, *one joint tenant cannot enfeoff his companion*, becauſe *his companion* has the feiſin already ; each joint tenant being feized *per mie et per tout*. But, as *tenants in common* and *coparceners* as to ſome purpoſes, have feveral freeholds, they *may* enfeoff their companions of their reſpective ſhares.

Gilb. Ten. 72.

See 1. *Burr.* 92.

But a feoffment by a perſon having no right of property in the lands is good, becauſe the moment he enters to give feiſin he gains the fee ſimple in poſſeſion by wrong.

This

This mode of conveyance is, in many Touchfl. 203. inftances, the moft advifable, as it clears all difícifins, &c. and turns all other eftates into rights, fo that a fine, levied by the See 2. Bl. Comm. 357. feoffor to the feoffee, or by the feoffee to r Salk. 340, a ftranger, will bar them, if not avoided & N. (b). 2 Lev. 52. within the time prefcribed by the ftatute.

The giving of livery, indeed, is often attended with inconvenience and expence when the feoffor refides at a diftance from the lands : but this may be eafily prevented by executing a power of attorney : and we may remember that corporations muft always make attornies, under their common feal, to deliver feifin.

· A feoffment therefore is incompatible with any conveyance operating by way of ufe. A feoffment and bargain and fale cannot be made by the fame perfon, of the fame lands, at the fame time ; for the feoffment conveys the feifin or poffefsion to the feoffee, while it is abfolutely effential to the efficacy of a bargain and fale that it remain in the bargainor. Now the poffefsion cannot be in,

H   and

and not in, the feoffor at the fame time. If the feoffment take effect, the poffef-fion *muft be out of him* by the very act of livery ; and if the poffefsion *be out of him*, he cannot be feized to the ufe of the bargainee. A bargain-and-fale is a con-tract to convey, and not an abfolute con-veyance as a feoffment. A perfon cannot contract to fell what he has actually parted with. If he conveys the poffefsion to another he can have none in himfelf to fupply the ufe.

2 Bl. Comm. 300.
Gilb. Ten. 133, & *Watk.* n. LIV.

A claufe of *warranty* is ufually added to a feoffment ; but it is preferable to in-fert a covenant by the feoffor, " for him-felf, his heirs, executors, and adminiftra-tors," as the warranty only binds the *heirs having affets.* Yet it may be fome-times prudent to infert a claufe of war-ranty in addition to the covenants, as it may pofsibly bind a reverfioner or re-mainder-man when no affets defcend,— and be even a bar to a latent entail.

CHAP.

CHAP. II.

─────────────

OF A GRANT.

A Grant is appropriated to the conveyance of things *not in pofsefsion*, as reverfions and remainders, and other incorporeal hereditaments, as rents, advow-
fons, &c. of which no livery can, of
courfe, be given. Hence the law divided
eftates into thofe which lay in *livery* and
thofe *in grant*.

2 *Bl. Comm.* 317. *Touchft.* 228. *Butl.* n. (1) to *Co. Litt.* 384. a. *Sand.* *Ufes.* 327.

As livery of feifin was a matter of noto-
riety, it was effential to the transfer of
whatever that livery could be made. It
was, indeed, of itfelf, fufficient to effectuate fuch transfer; and no farther evidence of the conveyance was required
than the evidence of fuch livery. But,
as livery could not be made of in-
incorporeal hereditaments, interefts, or
rights, the law, even before the ftatute

of

of frauds, required the transfer of them to be in writing under feal. In many *Gilb.Ten.*81. cafes alfo, it ordained that *attornment* fhould be made; as in the conveyance of a reverfion or a feigniory ; and that for the following reafons :

1ft, That the tenant in poffefsion might not be fubjected to a ftranger, or a new lord, without his own approbation and confent.

2dly, That he might know to whom he was to render his fervices, and diftin-guifh the lawful diftrefs from the tortious taking of his cattle.

3dly, That by fuch attornment the grantee of the reverfion or feigniory might be put into the poffefsion of it, and that others might be apprized and informed of the transfer.

The reafons, however, for attornment having, in a great meafure, ceafed from the change of manners, and the decline

of

of feudal principles, attornment is now *Stat.* 4. *Anne*
rendered unneceffary to the completion *C.* 16. *S.* 9, 10,—& 11.
of a grant. *Geo.* 2. *C.* 19. *S.* 11.

The operative word in this fpecies of
conveyance is " grant.".

CHAP.

CHAP. III.

OF A GIFT.

2. *Bl. Comm.*
316.
Touchft. 227. A Gift is, properly, a *voluntary convey-ance*; that is, a conveyance *not founded on the confideration of money or blood.*

The operative word in it is " *given.*" It is, at this day, a fufpicious fpecies of conveyance, as being without what the See 13. *Vin.* law denominates either a good or valu-519. Fraud. 22 *Vin.* 15. able confideration. It is void as to Voluntary Convey. thofe who were creditors of the donor at the time of it's being made, though valid as to fubfequent creditors. If it be of an eftate in poffefsion, it re-quires livery to perfect it : For, as it has no confideration either of blood or mo-ney, no ufe arifes on it ; and, confe--quently, livery is ftill neceffary.

Originally

Originally feoffments were confidered 2. *Bl. Comm.* 310. as gifts. The term Gift now, however, is generally appropriated to the creation of an *eftate tail:* hence the perfon creating an eftate tail is denominated the *donor,* and the perfon taking it the *donee:* hence the iffue of a tenant in tail is faid to take *per formam doni,* and the *F. N. B.* 211, 212. writ given him to recover his eftate is called the *formedon.*

CHAP. IV.

OF A LEASE.

2. *Bl. Comm.*
317.
Touchst.
Ch. 14.
*Bacon on
Leases,* & *Ante*
b. 1. c. 2.

Litt. S. 459.
Co. Litt. 270.

A Leafe is the grant of the poffefsion of lands, or other things, to a perfon for *life, years,* or *at will.*

On a leafe for life, as it goes to the feifin as well as to the poffefsion, livery muft be made, as on a feoffment; unlefs it be created by way of ufe, or devife. A leafe for *life,* therefore, is a *freehold* intereft, and muft be paffed by livery, &c. as any other eftate of freehold. But a leafe for *years,* pafsing only the right of *pofsefsion* as contradiftinguifhed from the *feifin,* is completed by *the entry of the lefsee;* for even *before* the entry, an *intereft* paffes to him (called his *interefse termini)* which the lefsor cannot refcind. *Before* entry, however, the lefsee cannot bring

bring an action of trefpafs; nor is he, till entry, if he takes at common law, and :not by way of ufe, capable of receiving a *releafe of the reverfion.*

A leafe for a chattel intereft is ftill good by parol, fo it exceed not three years from the making ; but, if it be for a longer term, or for an eftate of freehold, it muft be by deed or note in writing, figned according to the ftatute of frauds.   29 *Car.* 2. *C.* 3.

A leafe is ufually and properly in confideration of a yearly rent; and the beft way of referving fuch rent is to referve it generally, as " yielding and paying, therefore, yearly, during the faid term, the fum, &c." as the rent fhall follow the reverfion.   See *Ante* b. 1. c. 22. (of rent).

A leafe may be *afsigned*; that is, the *whole intereft of the lefsee* may be conveyed to another ; or the leffee may *underlet*, that is, convey for *a lefs term* than he himfelf has in the lands. If, therefore, it is intended, that he fhall not do fo, an exprefs provifion   2. *Bl. Comm.* 326, 7. *Dougl.* 187. N. (*) 59. Palmer *v.* Edwards. 1. *Str.* 405, Poultney *v.* Holmes. *Dr. & Stud.* 1 *Dial.* 1. c. 8.

2. *Stra.*1221. provifion or covenant fhould be inferted to
Lekeux *v.*
Nafh.   reftrain him.   But this covenant does not
* 3 *Bro. C.C.* come within what the law denominates
632.Hender-
fon *v.* Hay. the *ufual covenants**.

. Again, a leffor is not obliged to renew
the leafe (unlefs by cuftom); and, therefore, if it be intended that the leffor
fhall be compelled to do fo, a covenant
2. *Bro. C. C.* for that purpofe fhould be alfo inferted.
636.
Tritton *v.* But if the leffor covenant to renew under
Foot.
3 *Ves. Jun.* " *the like covenants,*" it will not extend
295.
Baynham *v.* *to a further covenant for renewal.*
Guy's Hofp.

*Co.Litt.*53.a. A leffee for years is compellable to re-
pair, &c. and, therefore, if it be not intended that he fhould do fo, a covenant
from the leffor fhould be inferted.

The operative words in a leafe are
" *demife, leafe, and to farm lett.*"

2. *Bl. Comm.* See *Ante,* book 1. ch. 2. of terms for
319, &c.
Touchft. 280, years.   And as to leafes by hufband and
&c.
Bac. on Leafes, wife of the wife's lands, ecclefiaftical per-
C.   fons, corporations, guardians, &c. the
books cited in the margin.

                                        CHAP.

CHAP. V.

___

OF AN EXCHANGE.

An Exchange is a *mutual* grant of 2 *Bl. Comm.* 323. *equal interefts*, the one in confideration of *Touchft.*C.16. the other. No livery was neceflary on an exchange at common law; but entry *Co.Litt.*50.b. *Perk.* S. 285. by each party was abfolutely neceflary to effectuate it.

If both parties die before entry, the exchange is void; and if one die, his heir may avoid it. Hence the beft mode of exchange (except as to corporate *Butl.*) n. (1.) to *Co. Litt.* 271. b. S. 3. bodies, or others who cannot ftand feized to an ufe,) is by a conveyance founded on the ftatute of ufes, as by leafe and releafe; which does away the necef- fity of entry.

An

3. *Wilf.* 483. An exchange can only be between
Hargr. n. (1)
to *Co. Litt.* *two parties,* though the *number of perfons*
50. b. is immaterial. The word " *exchange* " is
the only operative word, and therefore
indifpenfible, and it implies a *mutual*
warranty.

CHAP.

CHAP. VI.

OF A RELEASE.

A RELEASE is the relinquifhment of a right or intereft in lands or tenements to another who has an eftate *in poffefsion* in the fame lands or tenements.

2 *Bl. Comm.* 324.
Gilb. Ten. 53.
Touchft. c. 19. p. 320.
Litt. Ch. 8. f. 444, &c.

There are five fpecies of releafe: 1ft, *by way of enlargement*; as if he in remainder in fee releafe to the particular tenant in poffefsion. 2dly, *By way of pafsing an eftate*; as when one coparcener or jointtenant releafes to the other. 3dly, *By way of pafsing a right*; as when a difieifiee releafes to the difieiffor. 4thly, *By way of extinguifhment*; as if my tenant for life makes a greater eftate than he is warranted in granting, and I releafe to his grantee; or if the lord releafe to his tenant his feigni-

feigniorial rights. And 5thly, *By way of entry and feoffment*; as when a diffeiffee releafes to one of two diffeiffors.

But, in order to give operation to a releafe, it is neceffary that the releafee have the feifin, or at leaft poffeffion, of the premifes, either by livery, by the ftatute of ufes, or by actual entry; and, therefore, if any convey by leafe and releafe, who cannot ftand feized to an ufe, as a corporation, the leafe on which the releafe is to be grounded muft not be in the common way of bargain and fale, but by way of demife and leafe at common law, *with actual entry by the leffee.*

Care muft alfo be taken that the premifes in the leafe, or bargain and fale, be at leaft commenfurate with thofe in the releafe, as the releafe is only of the right to, or eftate in, the premifes of which the releafee is in actual poffeffion; and, confequently, no more can pafs.

A releafe is the proper mode of extinguifhing or conveying a right to, or an
equity,

equity, or contingency, or possibility, in the lands of the releasee.

The operative words in a *release* are, " *remise, release, and for ever quit claim and discharge.*"

CHAP. VII.

OF A CONFIRMATION.

2 *Bl. Comm.*
325.
Gilb. Ten. 75.
Touchft. 311.
Litt. ch. 9.
f. 515, &c.

A CONFIRMATION differs effentially from a releafe, as it only validates and eftablifhes that eftate or intereft which the tenant *already has*; whereas a releafe is the relinquifhment of a right which the tenant had not before. So far as the particular eftate is *increafed*, it is *not* a confirmation; it is not the *ftrengthening of the tenant's eftate*, but the *giving him a greater one*.

The operative words are, " *ratified and confirmed* ;" though, from fafety, it is ufual and prudent to infert the words, " *given and granted*," alfo.

CHAP.

CHAP. VIII.

OF A SURRENDER.

A SURRENDER is the yielding up, or returning, or relinquilhing, of *a fmaller eſtate*, to him who has a *greater eſtate* in the fame lands, in remainder or reverſion *immediately expectant upon ſuch ſmaller eſtate:* for if there be an eſtate to *A.* for life, remainder to *B.* for life, remainder to *C.* in fee, *A.* cannot ſurrender to *C. by reaſon of B.'s mediate or intervening eſtate.* If *A.* paſs his eſtate to *C.* it will *not be a ſurrender*, any more than if made to a ſtranger who had nothing in the lands.

2 *Bl. Comm.* 326.
Touchſt. ch. 17. p. 300.

As a ſurrender is, generally, for the advantage of the ſurrenderee, the law will often preſume his aſſent to it; for the particular tenant cannot enforce it upon him *nolens volens*, and ſo get rid of his obliga-

I   tions:

tions: but it is always prudent to make the furrenderee a party, and exprefs his confent, that it may be apparent on the very face of the deed.

A furrender might have been by parol ; but now, by the ftatute of frauds, it muft be by deed or note in writing.

Sand. Ufes. 36a.   The operative words in a furrender are, " *furrendered and yielded up* ;" though they are ufually preceded by the word " *granted.*"

CHAP.

CHAP. IX.

OF AN ASSIGNMENT.

A N Afsignment is, properly, the trans- 2 *Bl. Comm.* 326. fer of one's whole interest in *any* estate; but it is now generally appropriated to the transfer of *chattels*, either real or perfonal, or of *equitable interefts*.

An *afsignment* of a term differs from an *Ante.* b. 2. *under-leafe*, in that the *former* is the part- c. 4. ing with the *whole*, and the *latter* with *a portion only, of one's intereft or eftate.*

The operative words are, " *afsigned, transferred, and fet over*;" though ufually the word " granted" is inferted; and, in the afsignment of *chattels*, the words " *bargained and fold*" alfo.

CHAP. X.

OF A DEFEASANCE.

2 *Bl. Comm.*
327.
Touchſt. ch.
22. p. 396. A DEFEASANCE is a collateral deed, made at the ſame time with a feoffment or other conveyance, containing certain conditions, upon the performance of which the eſtate then created may be defeated or totally undone.

A defeaſance is now, however, ſeldom reſorted to, as it is much preferable to make the conditions apparent in the deed, ſo that the deed ſhall be complete in itſelf.

CHAP. XI.

━━━━━━━━━

OF A COVENANT TO STAND SEIZED.

A COVENANT to ftand feized to the ufe of another muft be *by deed*; for a covenant cannot be by *parol.* It muft be by a perfon *feized* of lands or tenements; and, confequently, cannot embrace an equity, or right, or contingency, &c. though it may be of a *reverfion*, or *vefted remainder*; for the reverfioner or remainder-man *is in the feifin.* It cannot be by a *corporation*; for a corporation cannot be feized to an ufe; or by a tenant in tail, except as to his own life. It muft be *in confideration of marriage* or *blood*; for a covenant to ftand feized *to the ufe of a ftranger* would be void. It muft *not* be in confideration *of money*; for that would be a bargain and fale. But it is not neceffary that the con-

2 *Bl. Comm.* 338. *Touchft.* 511, 512. *Sand. Ufes.* 556. See alfo *Com. Dig. Cov.* (G.)

I 3   fideration

fideration of blood be *expreſſed*; the nam-
ing the covenantee or *ceſtui qui uſe* as the
wife, ſon, &c. of the covenantor, is enough.·
A perfon may covenant to ſtand feized to
an ufe *in futuro,* as from Chriſtmas next;
or, if he be feized in fee-fimple, that his
heirs ſhall ſtand feized after his deceafe.

. The proper word is " covenant;" but
other words may be tantamount; as, if a
perfon " *bargain and ſell* " in confideration of *blood* or *marriage,* it will be good
as a covenant to ſtand ſeized.

As foon as the ufe is raifed, it is executed
by the ſtatute without any enrollment,
though the ufe be in fee.

CHAP.

CHAP. XII.

―――――

OF A BARGAIN AND SALE.

A BARGAIN and Sale differs from the covenant to ſtand ſeized, as it muſt be in *conſideration of money*, though that conſideration be only nominal. If the uſe to be raiſed by it be for *a freehold intereſt*, it muſt be *enrolled*. In this, as in the laſt ſpecies of conveyance, there muſt be *a perſon to ſtand ſeized*; and, therefore, in the caſe of a corporation, ſome other mode ſhould be adopted. There muſt be *an eſtate* in him of which he has the *ſeiſin*, as an *eſtate of freehold in poſſeſsion, reverſion, or remainder*; not a *mere right, contingency, or poſsibility*; and there muſt be a *perſon capable of taking the uſe.*

The operative words are, "*bargained and ſold.*"

2 *Bl. Comm.* 333. *Touchſt.* c. 10. *p.* 221. *Sand. Uſes.* 404.

CHAP. XIII.

OF A LEASE AND RELEASE.

2 Bl. Comm.
339.
Sand. Ufes.
461.
Butl. n. (1)
Co. Litt.
271. b.

WE have already remarked, that a re-leafe can only be made to a perfon in the poffefsion or feifin of the lands; and, therefore, if a conveyance of the freehold is intended to be made to a ftranger, with-out the formalities of livery, an eftate for a year, or other definite time, may be made to him in order to give him fuch poffefsion or feifin, and fo make him ca-pable of receiving a releafe. This may be done by a conveyance at common law, or under the ftatute of ufes.

If an eftate for a year be granted at common law, the leffee fhould make *an actual*

actual entry into the lands before the releafe be made to him; and this fhould always be done when a corporation is the grantor, as a corporation cannot be feized to an ufe. If, however, the grantor can ftand feized to an ufe, he may, to avoid the trouble of an actual entry by the grantee, make a bargain and fale, in confideration of money (though for a nominal fum only, as for 5s. which is never intended to be paid), to the purchafer for a year: an ufe then arifes which the ftatute immediately executes without enrollment; and, when the purchafer is thus in poffefsion or feifin (for a bargain and fale may be made as well of a reverfion or vefted remainder as of an eftate of freehold in poffefsion), a releafe may be made to him.

Butl. n. (3) to *Co. Litt.* 270. a.

The proper words in the inftrument on which the releafe is to be grounded are, if the inftrument is intended to operate *as a leafe with entry,* " *demifed, leafed, and to farm letten* ;" if otherwife, " *bargained and fold.*"

In

In the former cafe, a rent fhould be referved, though it be a nominal one only;
as a pepper-corn, if demanded. In the
latter cafe, the refervation is not material,
as the confideration of 5s. is fufficient to
raife the ufe.

CHAP.

CHAP. XIV.

OF A DEVISE.

S.UCH are the principal inſtruments of conveyance which are amicable and not forenſic, and to take effect in the maker's life-time; what we are now to ſpeak of is a voluntary conveyance, but not to take effect till the maker's death. Till that time it may be altered or revoked, either expreſsly or by implication. It is, as the law terms it, *ambulatory* till the teſtator's deceaſe. Though it does not receive its conſummation till the death of the teſtator, yet it ſhall relate, as to ſome purpoſes, to the time of its being made.

It cannot embrace any freehold property which was not in the teſtator at the time of its publication. If the teſtator, there-

2 *Bl. Comm.* 373. *Powell on Deviſes.* *Touchſt.* c. 23. p. 399. &c.

therefore, afterwards purchafe lands, or do any act which might be conftrued into a revocation of fuch will, care fhould be taken to have it republifhed.

The fame ftrictnefs of exprefsion is not of necefsity in wills as in deeds, with re-fpect to limitations, &c. but, in the making of wills, too much care cannot be taken in purfuing thofe defcriptions which the law has given, and in ufing technical terms in a technical fenfe.

Statute of Frauds, 29 *Car.* II. *c.*3.   A devife of freehold lands need not be under *feal* as a deed, but muft be in writing, and figned by the party devifing, or fome other perfon in his prefence and by his exprefs directions, and attefted and fubfcribed, in the prefence of the devifor, by three or four credible witneffes.

CHAP.

CHAP. XV.

***

OF A FINE.

A FINE is the compromife of a fictitious fuit, and operates either by pafsing an intereft, or by way of eftoppel.

2 *Bl. Comm.* 348. *Touchft.* c. 2. p. 2. *Cruife on Fines.* *Hargr.* n. 1. (C.) to *Co. Litt.* 121.a.

In order to pafs an intereft, the cognizor or cognizee muft have an eftate of *freehold* in the premifes, either in poffefsion, remainder, or reverfion, or be *ceftui que truft* in tail or in fee; for, otherwife, a perfon not bound by eftoppel might vacate the fine by pleading *partes fines nihil habuerunt.* But whether the freehold be in the cognizor or cognizee, either by right or by wrong, is of no confequence; and hence, when a fine is to be levied in order to ftrengthen a title, *a feoffment* may often be neceffary, as the cognizor or cognizee

would

would then, at leaft, have the freehold in him *by diffeifin*.

If there be no intereft in the perfon levying the fine, none can of confequence pafs. The fine, in that cafe, if it operate at all, can only operate *by conclufion or eftoppel*.

All *parties* to a fine, whether any intereft pafs or not, are concluded, as every one fhall be concluded by his own deliberate act.

Hob. 333. *Privies* (who are alfo eftopped) are either privies *in eftate*, as the donor and donee; *in blood*, as the heir and anceftor; or *in law*, as the lord and tenant, &c.

Strangers to a fine are all perfons who are neither parties nor privies.

In order to bar an eftate tail by fine, the privies muft be privies *in eftate*; that the iffue be privies in blood only is not enough. The iffue, to be barred by a fine, muft claim *the eftate* from the perfon levying it, or derive his title through him.

If

If lands, therefore, be given to *A.* and the heirs *female* of his body, and he have a fon and daughter, and the *fon* levy a fine and die, the daughter fhall *not* be bound; for though fhe be heir to the fon, and fo privy *in blood* to him, yet fhe is *not* privy to him *in eftate*, as fhe does not claim it from or through him. But if lands were given to *A.* in tail general, and his eldeft fon, in the life-time of *A.* levy a fine, the entail will be barred on the death of *A.* whether the fon furvive him or not; for the iffue of *A.* will be privies both in blood and eftate to *A.'s* eldeft fon.

If *a contingent remainder* be limited to *A.* in tail, and, before the contingency happen, he levy a fine, his iffue fhall be barred; for though *A.* was never *feized* of an eftate of freehold in the lands fo en-tailed, yet, as whoever claims fuch lands by virtue of the entail muft claim *from him* as the firft taker, they muft be privies both in blood and eftate to him, and fo be bound by the ftatute.

1 *Fearne,*535.

So

1 *Fearne*,521.
& fee *Butl.*
n. (1.) to *Co.*
Litt. 191. a.

So if lands be given to *A.* and *B.* and the heirs of the body of the furvivor, and they *join* in levying a fine, the entail will be barred; as the iffue, who would claim the entail, muft be privy both in blood and eftate to one or other of them; and they were *both* bound by the fine.

2 *Cruife*, 163.
3 *Co.* 72.

So to hufband and wife and the heirs of their two bodies, and the hufband alone levy a fine;- the iffue would, at leaft before the ftatute 32 *Hen.* 8. *c.* 28. *f.* 6. have been barred, as they muft be privy both in blood and eftate to the hufband as well as to the wife.

2 *Cru.* 162.

A widow is prohibited by ftatute from levying a fine of lands moving from her hufband.

A fine is no bar to a remainder or reverfion which is in another perfon, fo he claim within the time prefcribed by the ftatutes; for the remainder-man, or the reverfioner, claims paramount the cognizor: but, if the tenant in tail have the reverfion in himfelf, he may pafs a clear fee. The operation of a fine, in the latter cafe, would be this:—The tenant in tail would,

would, by fuch fine, pafs a *bafe fee* to the cognizor, derived from the eftate tail, and alfo a clear and abfolute fee of which he was feized in reverfion; and, as two fees cannot fubfift together in the fame perfon, the bafe fee fhall merge in the abfolute one, which would, confequently, come immediately into poffefsion.

1 Salk. 338. Symonds v. Cudmore.

5 Durnf. & Eaft. 109. note.

But as a tenant in tail may *charge* his reverfion with leafes, debts, &c. care muft frequently be taken how the reverfion be brought into poffefsion, as the charges would immediately attach. It may, therefore, often be prudent to fuffer *a re-covery*; which would give a new fee not fubject to thofe charges. But, even in the cafe of a recovery, the eftate will be chargeable *as to the acts of the recoveree himfelf*, upon the principle that no man fhall be permitted to defeat his own charges by an act of his own. A recovery, there-fore, only lets in the charge of *the perfon fuffering it*, while a fine will let in the charges of *the anceftors feized of the reverfion*, *as well as thofe of the cognizor.*

Cru. on Fines. 274.

Cru. on Recov. 284.

K   As

As a recovery immediately bars remainders over in another, which a fine will not do, as well as prevent the charges of the anceftor of the recoveree from attaching, it is generally the moft effectual affurance. A fine, however, is fometimes the preferable one, and often the only one to be adopted.

A fine will, in certain cafes, bar *by eftoppel* where a recovery will not do fo. A fine may be levied of an entail *in remainder* without the concurrence of the perfon having the freehold; but a recovery cannot be fuffered but by the act of the perfon having *the freehold in poffcffion.*

1 *Cru.* 151.
3 *Co.* 86. a.
&c.
But, in order to *bar* an eftate tail, whether in poffefsion or remainder, the fine muft be with *proclamations*, according to the ftatute; for otherwife it will only work *a difcontinuance.*

Hargr. n. 1.
(C.) to *Co.*
Litt. 121. a.
A fine bars a married woman, it being a matter of record, as the compromife of a fuit; and, in levying it, the woman is examined apart from the hufband, that any

any compulfion on his part may, as much as pofsible, be avoided. A fine, therefore, is effential to give validity to her convey-ance of freehold lands (except where a recovery is required*), and is moft com-monly levied for the purpofe of barring her claim to dower.

* *Plowd.* 514. Eare *v.* Snow.

As an ufe immediately arifes on a fine, fuch ufe is immediately executed by the ftatute, and may be led or declared as the parties pleafe.

CHAP. XVI.

OF A RECOVERY.

2 *Bl. Comm.* A S a Fine is the *compromise* of a fictitious
357.
Touchst. c. 3. fuit, fo a recovery is a fictitious fuit *carried*
p. 37.
Pig. on Recov. *on to judgment.*
2 *Cruise.*

By the common law, the perfon who
had the immediate freehold, or freehold
in poffefsion, was to anfwer the claims of
ftrangers. Againft him the writ, or *præcipe*,
was brought. Hence, to this day, no recovery can be fuffered, unlefs *the recoveree*
has the freehold in pofsefsion in him; as the
recovery, or fuit, is founded on the *præcipe*,
which can only be fued out againft *the*
tenant of the freehold.

A perfon, therefore, who has an eftate
tail *in remainder*, cannot fuffer a recovery
alone;

alone; the tenant of the particular estate
of freehold in poffefsion muft concur, a-
gainst whom, or against whofe alienee, the
præcipe muft be brought; and the remainder-man muft come in *by voucher*. A recovery may, indeed, be now fuffered of a a 2 *Cru.* 239.
trust estate, without the concurrence of the
perfon in whom the legal estate is vefted;
but this is only from necefsity, and to
preferve an analogy in the affurance, or
mode of deftroying an estate tail.

The perfon *against whom* the writ is
brought is called the *tenant*, as he was always *the immediate tenant of the freehold.*
The perfon *suing the writ* is called the *demandant*, as he *claims* or *demands* the premifes as his right and inheritance, alleging
that the tenant had *disseized* him, or at leaft
had come in *under* the *disseizor*, or in *the
post*. The tenant then *calls on the remainder-
man*, or *the perfon under whom he claims,
to warrant his title*, which is denominated
vouching the perfon, who is thence called
the *vouchee*. The vouchee either vouches
over, or makes default. On default made,
judgment is given that the demandant re-

cover

cover againſt the tenant, and that the
tenant recover againſt the vouchce or war-
ranter, and ſo on, which is called the *recovery in value*, or *recompence*, and is always ſuppoſed to go *as the lands would
have gone if they had not been recovered.*

When the *præcipe* is brought *immediately
againſt the tenant in tail*, it only bars him
of the eſtates of which *he is then actually
ſeized*. It is, therefore, uſual for him to
convey an *eſtate of freehold to another perſon*, that the *præcipe* may be brought a-
gainſt ſuch perſon (who is called *the
tenant to the præcipe*), *and that ſuch perſon
may vouch the tenant in tail*; for if the
tenant in tail comes in as *vouchee*, it bars
every latent right and intereſt which he
may have in the lands.

If the *præcipe* be brought *immediately
againſt the tenant in tail*, and he vouches
over the *common vouchee*, it is called a recovery with *ſingle voucher*; if againſt *the
tenant of the freehold*, and he vouch over
the tenant in tail, and *the tenant in tail vouch*
over

over the common vouchee, it is called a recovery with *double voucher*; and fo on, according to the number of perfons vouched.
And it is always proper to fuffer a recovery with at leaft a double voucher, if an
entail is to be barred, for the reafons before alleged.

A recovery bars not only an eftate tail, *Ante.* b. z.
but all remainders or reverfions expectant *c.* 15.
upon it if they are not in the crown.

The recoverer always gains a clear and
abfolute fee on his recovery of the premifes, not fubject to any charges but to
thofe of the recoveree. Hence it is preferable, in fome cafes, to a fine, though .
a fine might bar the eftates, as a fine lets
in the incumbrances of the anceftors as
well as thofe of the cognizors. In fome
inftances, however, a fine is preferable to
a recovery, as the former is *an eftoppel* by *Pig. Recov.*
the ftatute, where a recovery would not 32—34—55.
eftopp. 2 *Cru.* 271.

K 4 A re-

A recovery may be fuffered by a tenant in fee-fimple, in order to ftrengthen the title. So as it is a fuit, in the progrefs of *Plowd.* 514. which a feme covert is fecretly examined, Eare *v.* Snow. it will bar her of her claim to dower.

PRINCIPLES

OF

CONVEYANCING, &c.

BOOK III.

OF CONVEYANCES WITH RESPECT TO PARTIES.

CHAP. I.

OF AN INFANT.

An Infant may *take by purchase*, as he may do any thing which is manifeftly for his advantage; and, if a feoffment be made, livery may be given to him in perfon, or even to another whom he fhall appoint as his attorney; though the appointment of an attorney by an infant is not valid in itfelf at law.

Co. Litt. 2. b.

1 Roll. Abr. 730. Enfant. (D.) pl. 6. See 3 Burr. 1794. &c.

But

Co. Litt. 2. b.   But he may wave fuch conveyance when he comes of age; or, if he do not then actually agree to it, his heirs may wave it after him.

Touchſt. 232.   All conveyances, however, *by* an infant,
Ibid. 7.
Cru. Fines,   are voidable by him or his heirs, except a
110.
Cru. Recov.   fine or recovery, which are only voidable
144.   during his minority.   All thefe convey-
3 *Burr.* 1794.
Zouch v.   ances are, neverthelefs, if they tend to his
Parfons.
               benefit, good till actually avoided ; but as
to fines, the affidavit of acknowledgement
by *dedimus poteſtatem* runs now, by rule
of court, that " the parties were of full
age;" and, before that rule was ordained,
the commifsioners were fubject to an attachment if they took the acknowledgement of an infant.   An act of an infant,
Zouch v.   which *cannot* be to his advantage, is void
Parfons. *ubi*
ſup.   *ipſo facto.*

Cru. Recov.   It was formerly the practice to petition
148.   the King for a privy-feal to enable an infant to fuffer a recovery; but this is now
difufed, and recourfe is had at this day
to an act of parliament.

An

An infant truftee or mortgagee may be ordered to convey even by fine, if not by recovery (See 3 *Atk.* 16.), by a court of equity, under the ftatute of the 7th *Ann.* cap. 19. and that act extends to the conveyance of copyholds.

1 Watk.Copyh. 63.

So an infant may, in fome cafes, exercife a power, as where he is *a mere inftrument*; but it fhould feem not otherwife.

Powell on Powers, 43— 54. & 1 *Ves.* 304.

And an infant may be bound by a fair and reafonable marriage-fettlement.

1 Bro. C. C. 152. Williams *v.* Williams.

A guardian may make leafes during the minority of his ward.

2 Roll. Abr. 41.*Garde.*(2.) *pl.* 4. *Bac.onLeafes.* B. & I. (f.9.) p. 138.

An infant may be feized to an ufe *.

* *Sand. Ufes.* 87.

And an eftate may be limited by *way of remainder*, or *of ufe*, or given *by devife*, to an infant *en ventre fa mere*; but an *imme-diate* grant to fuch infant would not be good, as it would be *in futuro*. In the cafe of a devife, the fee defcends to the teftator's heirs at law till the child is born; in that of the remainder, the freehold is

See of the Stat. 10 & 11 *Willm.* III. N.(3.) to *Co. Litt.*298.a. & *Watk.on Defc.* ch. 4.

in

in the particular tenant; and the remainder vefts in the child, though unborn, by the ftatute 10 & 11 *Will.* III. and in the cafe of the ufe the legal eftate is in the truftee.

CHAP.

CHAP. II.

OF HUSBAND AND WIFE.

As the Hufband and Wife are but one
perfon in law, if an eftate be limited to
them, they fhall not take as joint-tenants
(for a joint-tenancy neceffarily implies a
plurality of perfons), but the entirety is
in each; and neither can alien without
the other. If it be limited to the hufband and wife and another perfon, that
other perfon fhall take a moiety in joint-
tenancy with the hufband and wife; and
the hufband and wife fhall have the other
moiety by entireties, as they are but one
perfon in law.

Litt. f. 291.
& *Co.* upon
that fect.
5 *Durnf. &*
Eaft. 652.
Doe v. Par-
ratt.
2 *Cru.* 213.

CHAP. III.

OF A FEME COVERT.

3 *Bl. Comm.* 292.
Touchst. 232.
A *FEME COVERT* may *accept* an eftate ; and it fhall be good till avoidance. But *her conveyance* is abfolutely void, and not merely voidable, except it be by matter of record. She can only be bound by fine, recovery, or act of parliament.

*Sand.Ufes.*88.
She may be feized to an ufe.

2 *Bl. Comm.* 318.
Bac. on Lea. (C.)
The hufband and wife, however, may together make leafes of the wife's lands for three lives, or a certain number of years, by the ftatute 32 *Hen.* VIII. *c.* 28.

Powell on Powers, 31. 42. *Hargr.* n. (6.) to *Co. Litt.* 112. a.
A power may be given to a married woman : and if a power be given to a *feme fole*, which it is intended fhe fhould

5   execute

execute though fhe afterwards marry, it
fhould be exprefsly faid " whether fole or
covert."

So a married woman may be enabled to 1 *Ves.* 303—
difpofe of her property, by limiting fuch 518.
3 *Bro.* C.C. 8.
property to her *feparate ufe*; in which
cafe fhe fhall be confidered in equity as a
feme fole.

So the hufband, on marriage, may give See 2 *Ves.*
612. &c.
the wife power to make a will, and it fhall
be good.

CHAP.

CHAP. IV.

━━━━━

OF THE KING. '

2. *Bl. Comm.* 346. S. 2. *Com. Dig.* Grant (G) 1. *Cru.* 98. 2. *Cru.* 144. *Pigg.* 74.

GENERALLY, the King cannot either grant or take but by matter of record ; as by deed enrolled. He may *take* by *fine*, though he cannot be a cognizor ; no^r can he be a party to a recovery, for the King cannot be fued.

*Sand.Ufes.*88.

Nor can the King be feized to an ufe.

Com. Dig. Grant (G) & Affignment. (D).

But the King may afsign certain things, as a *chofe en action*, &c. which the fub-ject cannot.

2. *Cru.* 255. *Com. Dig.* Eftates. (B. 31.)

A recovery by the fubject cannot af-fect the iffue in tail or any remainder, when the ultimate remainder or reverfion is in the crown.

CHAP.

CHAP. V.

─────────

OF THE QUEEN.

THE Queen may alien and purchafe without the concurrence of the King. She may levy a fine, as any other fub-ject: but it is faid, that fhe cannot be feized to an ufe.

CHAP: VI.

─────────

OF CORPORATIONS.

OF their capacity to take.   See 1 *Bl. Comm.* Chap. 18. 478-9.

Davys's Rep. 44. b.   Grants by Corporations muft be by deed under their common feal ;. and fuch deed, fo fealed, is good without delivery.

1. *Salk.* 193.   But they may bind themfelves by a matter of record without their feal.

Coke's Read. on Fines. Read. 7 & 8. 1. *Cru.* 118, 178.   Corporations *aggregate* cannot levy a *fine*, as they can only appear by attorney ; and a fine muft be levied in perfon. Though it is faid that a corporation *fole* may be a cognizor, for he may appear perfonally : but corporations of either kind may be *cognizees.*

4   But

But a corporation cannot be feized to an ufe; and, therefore, it cannot covenant to ftand feized, or make a bargain and fale. See *Sand. Ufes.* 446, & *Ante* b. 1. ch. 20.

And, therefore, if a leafe and releafe be made by a corporation, the inftrument, on which the releafe is to be grounded, muft not have the words—" doth: *bargain and fell*," but thofe of "*grant and demife*:" as it muft operate as a *leafe*, ftrictly, and *not as a bargain and fale:* and on fuch leafe, *the lefsee muft actually enter into the lands;* for, before entry, he can have no poffefsion on which the releafe can operate.

Ecclefiaftical corporations are reftrained from aliening, except for certain terms, by ftatute. 2 *Bl. Comm.* 320, 1. *Bac. Leafes.* E. F. G. H.

THE END.

London : Printed by G. Woodfall, No. 22, Paternofter-Row.

Lately publiſhed, by the ſame Author:

I. An Essay towards the further Elucidation of the Law of Descents.

II. An Enquiry into the Title and Powers of his Majesty as Guardian of the Duchy of Cornwall during the late Minority of its Duke.

III. Reflections on Government in General, with their Application to the British Constitution.

IV. The Law of Tenures; by the late Lord Chief-Baron Gilbert; with an Historical Introduction on the Feudal System, and copious Notes and Illustrations.

V. A Treatise on Copyholds; in two Volumes: Vol. I. containing the Doctrine of *Manors, Grants, Surrenders, Entails, Remainders, Executory Interests and Trusts, Admissions, Fines, Forfeitures, Extinguishment and Suspension, and Enfranchisement.*—Vol. II. *Courts, Customs, Freebench and Curtesey, Guardianship, Licence, Heriots, Suit, Rents, Corporal Services,* and the Application of *the Statute Law to Copyhold Property.*

VI. An Enquiry into the Question, *whether the Brother of the paternal Grandmother shall succeed to the Inheritance of the Son, in preference to the Brother of the paternal Great-Grandmother?* The Affirmative having been advanced by Mr. Justice Manwoode, acceded to by Mr. Justice Harper, Mr. Justice Mounson, and the Lord Dyer; and adopted by Lord Bacon Lord Hale, and the Lord Chief Baron, Gilbert; and the Negative maintained by Mr. Robinson, (the late Chief Justice of Gibraltar) and Mr. Justice Blackstone.

Lately publifhed,

1.

A TREATISE

ON THE

LAW OF EXECUTORS AND ADMINISTRATORS.

BY S. TOLLER, ESQ;

Price 8s. Boards.

2.

THE MODERN PRACTICE

OF

LEVYING FINES AND SUFFERING RECOVERIES.

BY WILLIAM HANDS.

Price 4s. 6d. Boards.

3.

SUPPLEMENT

TO

VINER'S ABRIDGMENT,

Volumes I and II.

Price 1l. 8s. Boards.

4.

ROPER

ON

THE LAW OF LEGACIES.

Price 4s. 6d. Boards.

5.

POWELL'S
LAW OF MORTGAGES.

NEW EDITION.

2 Vols. 18s. Boards.

6.

POWELL'S
LAW OF POWERS.

Price 10s. 6d.

This Day is published,

Price 10s. 6d. Boards,

A

TREATISE

ON THE

CONSTRUCTION OF THE STATUTES
13 El. c. 5. and 27 El. c. 4.

RELATING TO

VOLUNTARY AND FRAUDULENT CONVEYANCES,

AND OF THE

NATURE and FORCE OF DIFFERENT CONSIDERATIONS,

To support DEEDS and other LEGAL INSTRUMENTS

IN THE

COURTS OF LAW AND EQUITY.

BY WILLIAM ROBERTS,

LINCOLNS INN.

———

LONDON:

PRINTED FOR J. BUTTERWORTH, FLEET-STREET.

Издание напечатано по технологии
Print-on-Demand (печать по требованию)
в одном экземпляре, по индивидуальному заказу.